STOP OVERTHINKING

BOOST YOUR SELF-ESTEEM TO OVERCOME ALL NEGATIVE THOUGHTS AND STAY MOTIVATED

JOHN WARD

John Ward

John Ward

a result of the use of the information contained within this document, including, but not limited to, — errors, omissions, or inaccuracies.

"Don't wait. The time will never be just right."

Napoleon Hill

CONTENTS

INTRODUCTION

Do you often get confused by your thoughts? Do you strive weekly with stress or anxiety about the things you need to fulfill? Do you just want to stop over-thinking life in general?

Now and then, we all experience negative thinking. But if you are still distracted by these feelings, then you can analyze carefully what you are thinking about and how your emotions affect your mental health.

This internal monologue is a regular part of your mentality. It's there all the time, night and day, continually telling you of the food you need to pick up, teasing you for skipping the birthday of your friend or making you feel nervous about current news (such as politics, the weather, or the current state of the economy). Such thoughts are your life's background noise, but you may not always be conscious of their relentless existence. Right now, take a second and pay close attention to your thinking. Try stopping your thoughts. It's tough, right? You can see how unbidden and sometimes unwanted they tend to flood in, one after another.

Some of your thoughts are obscure and unnecessary. "My arm is itching." "It looks like it's going to rain." Many of our emotions are distracting and pessimistic, on the other hand. "That guy is a jerk." "I screwed this project." "I am so culpable about what I said to Mama." Those thoughts clutter us, whether neutral, positive, or negative, just as your bedroom can be cluttered if you have too many personal belongings. Unfortunately, it is not so easy to clear up the mental clutter as it is to remove possession. You cannot "throwaway" a thought and wait for it to go down. Actually, like an endless Whack-a-Mole game, your negative thoughts will emerge as soon as you grope them down.

Now, envision in your mind a fully coordinated home – a home free from foreign, draining, and unnecessary objects that will agitate you. What if you can only surround yourself with ideas that lift, encourage, and ease you? Imagine your mind for a moment as a beautiful cloudless sky, and you have the freedom to choose what you want. If that bright mental sky is so ideal, why do we worry so much about random and unwanted thoughts with so few filters?

The brain has about 100 billion neurons, while the spinal cord comprises another billion. The cumulative number of interactions between neurons – the thinking cells – has been calculated to be 100 trillion. Our powerful brains actively process and evaluate all kinds of experiences in the form of thoughts. Thoughts shape what we see as truth.

We can regulate and direct our thoughts, but our thoughts sometimes feel as if they have their minds. They influence us and how we think. The idea is necessary to solve the problems, evaluate, determine, and prepare. Still, in the meantime, the mind roams like a wild monkey; it drags you through the thorns of negativity and rumination. Your daily inner conversation, right here and now, takes the focus away from you and from what is happening.

Absurdly, we believe that we have to think more or harder to 'work out' why we're not as glad or happy as we want to be. We seek to find assets, people, and interactions that can quench our desires and relieve our unhappiness. The more we think about our despair, the more we become despondent. Our minds make us anxious, hollow, and chaotic as we prepare for the future or look to the past for answers.

Indeed, almost every negative thought you have to do with the past or the future. It is normal to be stuck in a circuit of regrettable thoughts and concerns, even when feeling desperate to avoid the endless tape in your head.

This complex thinking or judging involves intense emotions. The more frightening, guilty, regrettable thoughts we have, the more stressed, worried, depressed, and frustrated we feel. The feelings often paralyze us with negative emotions, and those feelings deprive us of inner peace and joy.

Even if our emotions are the source of too much distress, you can't just stop thinking, right? You cannot shut your brain off at will or get rid of the mind chat and associated feelings that prevent you from truly enjoying life.

Now and then, we have natural inner calm and quiet moments. However, we seek to soothe mental debate more often by using too much food, alcohol, narcotics, work, sex, or exercise as self-medication. However, these are short-term solutions for noise muffling and pain relief. Our minds return to it soon enough, and the cycle continues.

Are we always bound to be accomplices of our "monkey minds"? Do we have to continue to battle our thoughts and let them weigh us down with guilt, remorse, and anxiety? Is there a way to have a pure, pain-free mind?

You may not always be able to keep your mind free from danger, but you may have ample effect on your outlook to boost your quality of life and overall happiness profoundly. Thinking may seem intuitive and uncontrollable, but many of our patterns of thought are regular and thoughtless.

While it seems integral to you and your feelings, you have a "conscious self" that can step in and control your thinking. You regulate your emotions even more than you think. When you start to adjust your mind, you open a path to the enormity of imagination, motivation, and ingenuity behind the untouched thoughts.

You will disable your thoughts and have more "space" in your mind to experience inner happiness and peace through practical habits and mindfulness practices. You will have the ability to determine what the essential thing in your life is, what no longer suits your goals, and how you want to live every day.

Many individuals overthink and over analyze every facet of their lives repeatedly, whether it is their careers, relationships, lack of success, or a relentless stream of stress. Almost all of these challenges in everyday life seem unavoidable.

Good habits such as meditation on consciousness, healthy relationships, and good sleep will take you to an environment where bad habits are lost. From unhealthy relationships to a cluttered living room, throwing away the reticence will give way to a whole new person, ready to face the challenges of life with a mind full of optimistic thoughts and concrete goals. I hope that you can understand your total capacity without feeling like overthinking every day, which means you can develop better habits. You can regain control.

This aim of the book is straightforward: I will educate you on the habits, actions, and thoughts that you can use to clean up the overthinking that could keep you from being more focused and conscious. Several books on this subject are available on the market; thank you once again for choosing this one. All attempts are made to guarantee that the knowledge is as useful as possible. Feel free to enjoy it.

MANAGE YOUR STORY

*O*verthinking is one of the most common mental conditions in the world, and unfortunately, it is also one of the most debilitating. You might think that it is no big deal, everybody gets lost in their thoughts sometimes, right?

Now, if you have any previous experience in falling into the almost endless spiraling pit of despair that is overthinking, then you know just how horrible it is. Overthinking can prevent you from enjoying the things that you used to love doing, like going to parties, walking in the park, or just meeting with friends. Overthinking can also negatively affect your performance at work, it makes you lose motivation, makes you procrastinate on your tasks, and thus ruining whatever chances of job progression you might have. Overthinking can also ruin your relationships; no one wants to be around a person who is always complaining, cranky, and has such a short temper so that you will have very few friends, and they might not be sticking around for much longer.

However, it seems like everything you do seems futile, it's as if there is always an insurmountable hurdle in front of you. Overthinking not only leaves you mentally drained, but it also makes you feel exhausted physically. It's like having an energy vampire latched permanently on your neck, and it is continuously feeding on what little mental and physical energy you have.

However, you should not lose hope just yet; there are plenty of ways that you can use to overcome your chronic overthinking problem. But first, you need to start with understanding the core problem; you need to know what overthinking is, and from there, you can start looking for the most viable solutions.

Everyone gets sucked into the rabbit hole of obsessive thoughts sometimes, and when it happens occasionally, then it is okay. However, when overthinking starts to consume your life, that is when it becomes a chronic mental problem.

Not everyone is prone to overthink, but some are more likely to suffer from it. For instance, people with a history of struggling with anxiety are almost always dealing with overthinking and its consequences daily. Overthinking is one of the triggers that cause stress in most people. Even if you do not have any history of mental health problems, if you consider yourself as a "problem solver" of sorts, then you are prone to overthinking. The thing you think as your most valuable asset, which is your analytical mind, can become your worst enemy when your overthinking is triggered.

If you are at a low point in your life where you have unusually high levels of uncertainty, it can trigger your overthinking disorder. Now that you have an idea of what overthinking is, the next thing that you need to know is the signs of overthinking to the lookout. Knowing the symptoms will inform you that you might need to be wary of the status of your mental health, maybe consider getting professional help. You can somehow gauge how deep into overthinking you are by identifying which symptoms have already manifested; if you find that you have signs of being a chronic overthinker, then you should probably consider getting professional help.

If you have trouble getting to sleep and you

cannot turn off your thoughts, even when you try, your thoughts start racing even faster when you try to stop them. All of these worries and doubts swirling in your head agitates you and prevents you from getting enough rest.

Overthinkers know the feeling of not getting enough sleep, almost too well actually. Insomnia happens because you have no control over your brain; you cannot shut off the chain of negative thoughts going through your mind at a hundred miles an hour. All of the things that worried you throughout the day come back just when you hit the sack, and you feel so wired that you cannot fall asleep.

If you are having difficulty calming your mind on your own, you can try different relaxing activities before you go to bed. There are plenty of things that might help you ease your mind just enough to let you get some sleep, like meditation, writing in a journal, adult coloring books, drawing, painting, reading a book, or even just having a pleasant conversation with a loved one. Do anything that can shift your attention away from the negative thoughts long enough for you to get some sleep.

Numerous medical researchers have discovered that most people suffering from overthinking disorders have turned to use recreational drugs, alcohol, overeating, or other ways to get a grip on their emotions somehow. Overthinkers feel the need to rely on external stimuli because they believe that their internal resources (aka their minds) are already compromised?

It is never a good idea to turn to try to treat yourself from overthinking. Odds are, you will still be overthinking afterward, and you have to deal with a different problem brought about by your self-medication.

If you are constantly feeling tired, you need to take action. Fatigue is your body's way of telling you to listen to it because there is something wrong going on; you should not ignore it and just hop from one activity to the next.

However, overthinking can also cause fatigue and exhaustion. Your mind is like a muscle; if you are continually burdening it with dozens of massive, negative thoughts all the time, and not even giving it some time to recover, it will get exhausted and cause you to burn out.

Back when humans were still living off the land, people did not have that many things to worry about, which means they do not have quite as many things to think about as well. In today's modern world, people lead complicated lives that require them to accomplish a lot of things in a short amount of time. In this fast-paced world, the need to slow down every once in a while is crucial for people's well-being. So, whenever you feel fatigued, or better yet, if you feel close to it, slow things down and figure out what your body, and your mind, needs before doing anything else.

Overthinkers have one major problem, and that is that they always feel that they need to be in control of everything. They plan out every aspect of their lives, some of them even go as far as planning up to the smallest detail. They feel that doing this is the only way they can feel safe, but it always seems to backfire at them because it is impossible to plan for everything that will happen in their lives.

Even so, they continue to plan out their futures, and they get anxious when unexpected things happen, and they always seem to be surprising things happening all the time. Overthinkers hate dealing with something that they do not have control over; they fear the unknown. When unexpected problems do surface, they cause them to sit and mull things over instead of taking immediate action to solve the unexpected issue. Numerous medical studies have shown that overthinking leads to making poor judgment calls, which is why over-thinking does not help.

When you catch yourself just before you start overthinking, try your best to bring your thoughts back to the present by taking deep breaths and thinking happy thoughts.

If you fancy yourself a perfectionist, and you often think about how awful you would feel if you were to fail somehow. This fear of failure can be so intense that it paralyzes you, and it keeps you from learning from your prior mistakes, which often lead to you repeating them.

Overthinkers often cannot accept failure, and they will do everything they can to avoid it. Ironically, they think that the only way not to fail is to do nothing at all. They mistakenly believe that to avoid failure, they should not put themselves in a position to fail at all, which also means they are not in the position to succeed as well.

If this sounds like you, remember that you are more than just your failures; no one could even remember the last time that you screwed up, it's just you. Also, keep in mind that it is impossible to escape failure, and you should never avoid it at all. For failure allows you to grow and evolve.

Instead of being excited about the things that you

are yet to experience, your anxiety and fear of what could go wrong paralyze you into doing nothing.

If you are afraid of what the future could bring, then your fear keeps you trapped inside your mind. Research shows that this fear of the future can be so crippling that sufferers tend to turn to drugs and alcohol so that they can tune out the negative thoughts that are clamoring inside their heads.

Tension headaches feel as if there is a thick rubber band wrapped around your temples, and it is slowly getting tighter. Aside from problems, you might also feel a sharp pain or stiffness in your neck. If you suffer from chronic tension headaches, it is a sign that you are overworking yourself, and you need a rest.

And by rest, it also includes rest from mental activities, like overthinking. Headaches are a sign that your body needs to take a break; this includes your mind. Even you might not notice it, but when you overthink, you are thinking of the same things over and over again.

Overthinkers usually have negative thought patterns that loop around themselves. To fight this, you need to break this loop by reinforcing positive thoughts. Take deep breaths, and focus your mind on every time your chest rises and falls, being mindful of the present will help you get rid of negative thoughts and the tension headache that came with them.

Stiff Joints and Muscle Pain- It might sound far-fetched, but overthinking can affect your entire body, not just your mind. And once your physical body is affected by your out of control negative thoughts, it will not be long until your emotional well-being gets hit too. Until you address and get rid of the under-lying issues that cause you to overthink, the body pains will continue. Overthinking might start in your mind, but its effects will gradually creep into the other parts of your body.

When you overthink, you will find it difficult living in the present moment and enjoy your life as it happens. Overthinking causes you to lose focus on the things happening around you; you are so engrossed at thinking about your problems. If your account gets bogged down by a ton of unnecessary thoughts, you are removing yourself from the present, and this can and will negatively affect your relationships.

You need to open yourself to the world around you; do not let yourself get too wrapped up in nega-tive thoughts. The only opinions that you should allow inside your mind are those that serve your well-being, ignore and forget about the ones that bring you down. There is so much beauty in life, and the opportunities for incredible experiences are unlimited. However, you can only appreciate them if you can manage to tune out the idle chatter in your mind and start listening to your heart instead.

DIFFERENT CAUSES OF OVERTHINKING

Again, there is nothing wrong about thinking about your problems so you can think of a solution for them, it becomes worrisome when you have a bad habit of twisting narratives around in your head until you can see every angle and side to it. Overthinking is not productive as it just makes you dwell over your problems; you are not looking for a solution for them, and you are only making yourself feel miserable

To find an effective way to break your over-thinking habit, you need to find out what caused it in the first place. Below are some of the more common reasons as to why people tend to overthink ;

If you are not self-confident, you tend to doubt every little thing that you say or do. When you hesitate, even a little, about the things that you want to do, you are letting uncertainty and fear creep into your mind, and it will be challenging to get them out of there. You can never really tell what your decisions will take you; even if you planned every little detail, the outcome will still not be what you hoped for (it could either be better or worse than what you expected).

It is only natural to worry when you encounter new and unfamiliar things and events. However, if you worry too much that you cannot even imagine a positive outcome, then it will trigger you to over-think. It is problematic because worry attracts even more problems, sometimes it creates ones out of thin air, which causes overthinking to go even deeper. Instead of mulling over how things could go wrong, it is better to entertain more positive thoughts, like how much better you would feel if a certain even turns in your favor.

Some people believe that they can protect them-selves from troubles whenever they overthink, but the truth is that overthinking is a trap that kills your progress. Overthinking and not doing anything to change the status quo might seem right, but stifling your development is never a good thing at all. Also, when you overthink, you are not staying in the same position, you are undoing whatever amount of progress you achieved thus far.

Many overthinkers became that way because

they cannot seem to get their minds off their problems no matter how hard they try.

Being a perfectionist is not necessarily a good thing. One could argue that being a perfectionist is not good at all. Most people who struggle with perfectionism are always anxious. They often wake up in the middle of the night, thinking of the things that they could have done better. Being a perfectionist causes overthinking because you are always trying to outdo yourself.

Reliance on quick fixes like with the advent of the internet also came a myriad of self-help videos, articles, and websites. The one thing that these resources promise is that they can help fix what ails you in a couple of easy steps. Of course, all of them are lying, but unfortunately, people usually have no other choice. However, many quick fixes do help, and that is the reason why it is problematic. Are you hungry? Just order a pizza or Chinese takeout using your phone. You do not like walking? Get yourself a car. Do you need to talk to your mother halfway across the country? Pick up your smartphone and start a video call. The modern world has so many quick fixes in place for almost every kind of problem that people might have. However, quick fixes just work most of the time, not every time. When a person's question remains unresolved for a few hours or even days, his mind automatically defaults to thinking that there must be something wrong, and this usually triggers overthinking.

For instance, if you are feeling upset for a couple of days, there must be some kind of quick fix for it. You think you need to quit your job, break up with your SO, stop talking to your parents; yes, these things might provide some form of cure for what ails you, but are these the correct choices, not necessarily. These options are Band-Aid fixes, not long-term solutions. And when these Band-Aid fixes eventually fail, people immediately fall into the spiral of overthinking.

When you feel stressed, the explanations that come to your mind are not the complete story. There are dozens of factors that might have contributed to your negative emotions, the things that you thought might be the reasons are just the tip of the iceberg. For instance, when you feel lethargic, you might think that it must be because you are unhappy with your job, or if you are having problems with your family, it does not even scrape your mind that you need more sleep because you are just skipping one hour of sleep. However, lack of sleep stacks up, and if you jump an hour of sleep every day for a week, your body will reflect all of the stresses that you have accumulated.

Western culture respects and encourages people to pursue their dreams. It can be positive, but when people believe that they can achieve their goals with little to no effort, that is when things go wrong. Most children grow up believing that they just need to be good little boys to get ahead in life, but then when they reach adulthood, the magic vanishes.

When a person first experiences the less than stellar world of the 9 to 5 office desk job, real relationship problems, and how incredibly bland and real healthy life is, they start to think of all the things that they might have done wrong for them to deserve their vanilla lives. When the gap between fantasy and reality becomes too high, it causes great sadness, which also causes them to give up on chasing their dreams.

For example, one person might think that there must be something wrong with the system because he did not get that promotion he worked hard to get, or why he is not feeling the effects of the economic boom that has been reported all over the news lately? It leads to even darker thoughts like maybe the reason he did not get that promotion was that he did not graduate from an Ivy League university. He starts blaming his parents for not paying for an Ivy League education. He also starts thinking that maybe it is his family that is holding him back from success, or perhaps the system at his work is rigged for him to fail. Or maybe, it is just that he is not as smart or as capable as his co-workers. All of these thoughts will start swirling around the person's head.

Although emotional awareness is still critical, you need to find a happy medium for it to become beneficial. The truth is that most men have ignored emotional awareness altogether, while most women have taken it a bit too far. It resulted in many women sitting and talking about their emotions. Still, rather than trying to fix their problems, this turns into an activity where they are just finding validation for their feelings. Not only is this kind of thing not helpful to your plight, but it can also be harmful and addictive. Rather than encouraging each other to take steps towards managing their emotions or solve their problems, they each stoke their fires, supporting themselves that their righteous indignation is justified and that there is nothing wrong with it.

Ignoring problems is terrible, but it also is taking self-awareness too far. People have become too introspective that even a twinge of sadness will trigger a rush of anxiety in them. Although some moods do hold messages, most of the time, their reasons are entirely inconsequential, like the horrible traffic on the way to work, or because you did not get enough coffee. People have become so hyper-vigilant about their emotions, and that alone is enough to fuel endless nights of overthinking.

2

LET GO OF THE PAST AND START BUILDING THE FUTURE

*H*ave you at any point felt pushed, restless, or overpowered by life? We live in a bustling world. With messages and messages flying all around as you are venturing over your kids' toys and attempting to get the canine sustained while the nourishment on the table is getting cold, you most likely get a handle on worrying constantly.

Mindfulness will enable you to diminish your pressure and nervousness, limit the measure of time that you spend feeling overpowered, and help you value every little minute as it occurs. In a universe of confusion, mindfulness may very well be the stunt you have to figure out how to have the option to adapt to the frenzy.

Luckily, there is a straightforward propensity

you can use to quiet yourself down and acknowledge life more usually. It's called mindfulness. Mindfulness is the act of deliberately concentrating the majority of your consideration on the present minute and tolerating it without judgment.

ADVANTAGES OF MINDFULNESS

Mindfulness diminishes Uneasiness; research has discovered that mindfulness is particularly useful in reducing nervousness. Rehearsing mindfulness revamps your cerebrum so that you can refocus your consideration. As opposed to following a negative and stressing thought down a way of every single imaginable result, you can figure out how to see the truth about your contemplations and simply let them go.

Mindfulness also improves memory, focus, and execution on the job. Mindfulness is one of the not very many strategies that function as a remedy for mind-meandering and the negative impacts that losing focus may have on you.

Mindfulness gives relief from discomfort, around 100 million Americans experience the ill effects of ceaseless torment each day, yet 40% to 70% of these individuals are not accepting legitimate medicinal treatment. Numerous investigations have demonstrated that mindfulness contemplation can decrease agony without utilizing endogenous narcotic frameworks that are generally accepted to diminish pain during subjective based systems like mindfulness.

Oneself created a narcotic framework that has, as a rule, been suspected of as the focal piece of the mind for mitigating torment without the utilization of medications. This framework self-produces three narcotics, including beta-endorphin, the met-and Leu-enkephalins, and the dynorphins. These work together to lessen pain by rehearsing mindfulness.

One of the most well-known manifestations that join tension is rumination or overthinking. After you start to stress over something, your mind will clutch that firmly and make it difficult to give up. It is anything but difficult to get into an idea circle where you keep on replaying every single awful result possible. We as a whole realize this isn't valuable since stressing over something doesn't keep it from occurring.

One investigation demonstrated that individuals who were new to mindfulness and started to rehearse it during a retreat had the option to give fewer indications of rumination and uneasiness than the control gathering.

Another advantage of mindfulness is in its impacts on the amygdala, which is the cerebrum's enthusiastic preparing focus. The unwinding reaction that your body needs to mindfulness reflection is a remarkable inverse of the pressure reaction. This unwinding reaction attempts to ease many pressures related to medical problems, for example, agony, wretchedness, and hypertension. Rest issues are regularly attached to these illnesses.

One investigation of more established grown-ups affirms that mindfulness contemplation can help in getting a decent night's rest. As indicated by this examination, mindfulness reflection can expand the unwinding reaction through its capacity to develop attentional components that confer command over the autonomic sensory system.

Mindfulness advances mental Wellbeing-Specialists have discovered that IBMT (integrative body-mind preparing) starts positive auxiliary changes in the cerebrum that could help secure against cerebral infection. The act of this strategy helps support productivity in a piece of the cerebrum that enables individuals to direct behavior.

Mindfulness advances intellectual adaptability; one examination proposes that not exclusively will mindfulness help individuals become less receptive;

it may likewise give individuals progressively mental flexibility. Individuals who practice mindfulness seem, by all accounts, to be ready also to rehearse self-perception, which consequently withdraws the pathways made in the cerebrum from earlier learning and permits data that is going on right now.

Mindfulness is not some practice limited to monks who have taken a vow of silence. It is the type of training that virtually anyone can do, at any time, and anywhere.

So, here are some additional strategies to implement mindfulness in your everyday life:

Sit with your experience at the point when you center on being careful, rehearsing mindfulness through concentrating on your body, psyche, and soul will enable you to turn out to be all the more dominant. The more you do this, the more you shut out the sense of self and the better you will feel in all pieces of yourself. Tune in for sounds that are close by or even far away. Output your body to get a feeling of what is loose and what is holding strain. If you have a tingle, see the tingle, however, don't attempt to transform it. Simply travel through it. It is an excellent practice for simply being careful without trying to take care of business.

Once in a while, life is awkward, like a tingle.

Sitting with the experience will enable you to see that things go back and forth. Nervousness can sneak up in your gut, or you may encounter a snugness in your throat while you reflect.

Mindfulness doesn't mean getting to be associated with the show of the psyche. It's tied in with seeing how the mind and body are reacting with full acknowledgment.

The touchy individual in you who has had numerous encounters will feel apprehensive, destitute, and desirous every once in a while. It is the mind and the conscience affecting everything. You are the caring person; you are the inhabiting being who knows.

To take advantage of the piece of you that sits looking out for this human experience, you simply need to remain completely focused. All of what I'm stating may appear to be exceptionally perplexing for some who have never polished mindfulness. It just requires some investment of not responding, and instead of watching your experience to comprehend the procedure, I'm discussing.

Reflection is an incredible practice for minutes that bring awkward feelings.

Make proper acquaintance with the one in your brain. Just inside, make a proper acquaintance. Who makes an appropriate acquaintance, and who hears him? It's you who's talking, and it's you who's tuning in.

The ideal approach to turn out to be free from the steady prattle that is bolstering your horrendous thoughts is to step back. Take a gander at it dispassionately. Musings are only an object of the psyche, something that should drift by and not be clutched or dismissed.

As you're careful and watch the voice, you'll start to see that the more significant part of what it says has next to no significance. It complains about the past and utilizes old encounters to attempt to control the present and future meetings. It causes a wide range of issues in your life.

If you need to turn out to be free from your brain, you must be careful enough to observe indeed what's happening up there. At the point when you discover that a lot of your activities originate from some nonsensical voice that wants comfort, you can start to settle on different choices.

All in all, mindfulness can mend numerous things, yet how would we accomplish it? One of the pathways to calm the psyche and go within ourselves is through contemplation.

Contemplation isn't tricky, but then its effortlessness threatens many. It is because your self-image wouldn't like to be calmed. It reveals to you that you're excessively occupied, that reflection is inconsequential, and that it's overly unusual and otherworldly for you.

What's truly going on is that the self-image is terrified of ending up calm. Backing off and going in methods, there's the capability of standing up to awkward sentiments. You gave your sense of self the activity of keeping away from distress or saw peril.

At the point when we ponder, there is an incredible danger of running into past torment.

Mindfulness, through your contemplation, enables you to at long last manage old injuries, so you don't need to live with them any longer. That implies that they never again have power over you.

To develop mindfulness, you'll need to invest significant energy consistently, yet this shouldn't be a task. The mind will prattle and reveal to you it's exhausted. Simply continue watching the objects of musings and emotions traveling through you.

The more you practice, the more you'll anticipate having that uninterrupted alone time. Consider it daily in the spa or getting a back rub. When you get into it, that focused inclination makes you feel as loose as 40 minutes in a sauna. While you'll start to experience benefits practically immediately, the more you practice mindfulness, the more unique the advantages will be in both the Buddhist ways of thinking and present-day psychotherapy. There is a wide range of approaches to reflect as well, so don't sit in lotus posture and consume those incense sticks at this time. Reflection is the umbrella for mending, and inside your contemplations, you can accomplish numerous things for the body, psyche, and soul.

Mindfulness contemplation isn't tied in with changing or modifying yourself in any capacity. It's tied in with getting to be mindful of what your identity is. As you sit peacefully, things will come up. As you search inside yourself, recollections may come up as if they are a motion picture on a screen. If you remain in the seat of cognizance without getting sucked in, you can become familiar with a great deal. You'll know if you get sucked in because you won't let pictures go. You'll get genuinely included, and pressure will begin to develop.

Buddha said that the wellspring of your enduring is attempting to flee from your direct experience. Remaining in a lovely minute from your past is equivalent to pieces of torment. Clutching things keeps you before, and it's mostly not beneficial for your mind.

COACHING TIPS:

- 1. To reduce and avoid overthinking, use validated techniques. Surprisingly, one of the simplest is the most effective. Distract yourself. Choose to turn your mind literally into something else, ideally absorbing and enjoying exciting and optimistic thoughts. Instead, many people find a stop sign and say either in their heads the word, "stop!" whenever the situation loudly requires it to be ruminated.

- 2. Offer yourselves to excellence. Learn to laugh at errors and challenges, welcome human error, and find irony and fun in it as it happens. Suppose people's lives are full and there are likely alternative explanations for what could be seen as a snub or power play otherwise. Realize that it's not about you most of the time.

- 3. Prevent causes. Keep away and limit your time to people or situations that lead you to feel depressed and think again as much as possible. Identify who and what and how your sensitivity to these stimuli can be reduced.

- 4. Go to "stream." Find areas of your life where you get so lost, whether it is playing the piano, shooting hoops, reading, walking, or kayaking. Schedule the stream times for events in your life every week, if possible, daily.

- 5. Learn, learn, practice, and practice! Ultimately, pick some of these tips, training, and practice. Study shows that it takes a lot of practice to "hardwire" a new habit, so be patient with yourself and just continue to use your unique strategies to turn your mind in an overthinking way. You should be both happier and more productive with time and practice.

You can practice a relaxation method like progressive muscle relaxation because people who display generalized anxiety often have high levels of responsiveness. Take up short-term activities that are captivating and enjoyable to take your mind off certain things and distract them from specific negative thoughts. These could be activities that have been useful in the past. An exercise is a vital tool for managing worry. When you exercise, brain chemicals are released that counteract low moods, fear, and anxiety. The practice also acts as a distraction from problems and reduces nervousness. Exercise at least once a day for half an hour, with cardio, exercises at least three days a week.

Incorporate organized problem-solving strategies to handle stressors that contribute to your worry. Everyone has problems and challenges in their lives, but they are more visible and challenging to handle if you always get worried. A useful strategy to combat this is training in organized problem-solving. Efficient problem-solving techniques minimize, reduce, control, and even prevent worrying in our daily lives.

Avoid activities and situations that foster anxiety by confronting your fears and facing them directly but gradually. For instance, you could place them in a hierarchy, depending on which step you fear the most. These fears could be: Arriving late for a meeting, Not checking your mobile phone for one hour, Going grocery shopping without a shopping list, Planning a birthday party, and accepting an invitation without checking with your calendar.

Well, as soon a person has been able to identify

and question his or her negative thoughts, then the next line of action is shifting attention away from the negative thoughts. Cognitive Behavioural Therapy assists in identifying and challenging these assumptions and helping individuals to develop alternative beliefs that are healthier and better for their well-being. Experiences have shown that mindfulness-based interventions will also aid you to remain focused.

Adopt Emotion Regulation and Mindfulness, recent studies have suggested that worry may present itself as a way of doing away with emotional processing. Involve yourself in what is called emotion-regulation strategies and mindfulness skills, as these will boost the form and manner in which you identify and experience underlying emotions.

Do away with the use of medications that will sedate you. Don't binge to relieve your anxiety. They may provide temporary relief from stress, but frankly, it will come back later. Instead of doing these, set up a time to consult a specialist or go for CBT if symptoms occur for longer than three months regardless of the above measures.

3

BECOME A PERSON OF ACTION

Finding a balance between thinking and acting is a challenge for many people, especially for those who are independent. How much time should you spend thinking versus acting? We hear advice all the time about creating plans for action, which implies that a careful collection of thoughts should govern all work. But then there is also the pressure to "Do It Now," which requires immediate action all the time and especially in these changing times of today.

How to know when to think vs. when to act What is the balance point between impulsive action and retardant thinking? It seems clear that the right balance of both is required, especially when you have your own business. However, the problem tends to yield to a small change in perspective. One that allows us to see that acting and thinking are much more similar than different. One of them is a physical action; the other is a mental action. I believe that the imbalance between thought and action is itself a symptom of a much larger internal inconsistency. You think you should achieve this balance when both things take you on different paths. You believe in one direction, but you act in another. It is easy to fall into a state of imbalance when you achieve a small change of perspective in your thoughts, but the inertia that you carry still guides your actions. In this way, you continue working under your old paradigms, but thinking within the framework of some new ones. It is only there, where you realize that thinking and acting are different things in themselves. You get results from both, but each takes you on slightly different routes, so it's easy to ask yourself which of the two paths is correct.

Overthinking might not seem so awful because thinking is excellent. Isn't that so? In any case, overthinking can cause issues. When you overthink, your decisions get overcast, and your pressure gets raised. You invest an excessive amount of energy in the negative, and it can wind up hard to act on it. On the off chance that this feels like a natural area to you, here are some straightforward plans to liberate your-self from overthinking. Occupy yourself into Joy, and once in a while, it is useful to have an approach to divert yourself with upbeat, positive, solid choices. Things like mediation, moving, working out, learning an instrument, weaving, drawing, and painting can separate you from the issues enough to close down the over-analysis.

You cannot have a remorseful idea and a thankful idea simultaneously, so why not invest the energy decidedly? Each morning and each night, make a rundown of what you are appreciative of. Get an appreciation for amigo and trade records, so you have an observer of the beneficial things that are around you.

Overthinking is something that can transpire. In any case, if you have an incredible framework for managing it, you can, at any rate, avert a portion of the negative, on edge, distressing thinking and trans-form it into something helpful, gainful, and successful.

It is, in every case, simple to make things more significant and more harmful than they should be. Whenever you find yourself preparing a specific mountain out of a molehill, ask yourself the amount it will matter in five years. Or on the other hand, so far as that is concerned, one month from now. Only this essential inquiry, switching up the period, can help shut down overthinking.

Before you can start to address or adapt to your propensity for overthinking, you have to figure out how to know about it when it is occurring. Whenever you wind up questioning or feeling pushed or restless, advance back and take a gander at the circumstance and how you are reacting, at that time of mindfulness is the seed of the change you need to make.

Confidence is a position of a riddle, where we discover the boldness to have faith in what we cannot see, and the solidarity to relinquish our dread of vulnerability. Each time I go into contemplation, it is a demonstration of trust, of squeezing into terror and drawing nearer to reality. Organize your shoulders and your feet level against the floor. Spot your hands over your kidneys (at your back under your lower ribs). Picture them and the little adrenal organs over them in your psyche. Furthermore, that is the place qigong contemplation steps in. By rehashing positive musings, you can make and fortify neural pathways, and clear up the kidneys, to assist you with more noteworthy authority over your feelings.

After a couple of breath cycles, lean forward a

little as you breathe in, catch your hands beneath your knees, open your eyes, and envision breathing out dread, making a "choo" sound. Close your eyes, grin, and breathe in your stomach out envisioning dull blue light and harmony encompassing your kidneys and adrenal organs. Breath out by driving your stomach back in.

Similarly, as with any feeling, contemplation can help balance out us, notwithstanding trepidation, to enable us to comprehend it all the more unmistakably. As the day progresses,

you can allow yourself to meet dread in an increasingly positive manner with the intensity of reflection. Check-in with your feelings consistently. At whatever point you feel dreadful, let the inclination remain. Rather than running, adopt a full breath and strategy your contemplations of fear and stress with neighborliness and interest. Be thoughtful to yourself in dread, as you would for a confided in a companion. If you have the opportunity and space, plunk down and inhale into your terror for ten breath cycles. Dread is stating that this is the ideal time to have the option to do what you're attempting to do. Your body is setting you up to have a positive result. When you can truly comprehend that dread is a feeling like some other feeling, you can figure out how to oversee it. And afterward, you can accomplish things that the vast majority consider to be exceptional. To beat my dread of statutes, I have grasped the fear, taking a lead shake climbing class where I need to move to the highest point of the divider and free fall mostly down the divider before being securely gotten with a rope. Through training, receptiveness, and cheering companions and teachers, I have figured out how to inhale through the dread and let go again and again.

Regardless of whether you are apprehensive because you have flopped previously, or you are frightful of attempting or over-generalizing some other disappointment, recall that since things did not work out, that does not imply that must be the result inevitably. Keep in mind, and each open door is a fresh start, a spot to begin once more. The dread that grounds overthinking is regularly situated in inclination that you are not sufficient or not savvy enough or persevering enough or devoted enough. When you have put forth a strong effort, acknowledge it in that capacity, and realize that, while achievement may depend to a limited extent on certain things you cannot control, you have done what you could do.

Give yourself a limit. Set a clock for five minutes and give yourself that opportunity to think, stress, and dissect. When the timer goes off, go through 5 minutes with a pen and paper, recording every one of the things that are stressing you, focusing on you, or giving you nervousness. Allow it to tear. At the point when the 5 minutes is up, toss the paper out and proceed onward ideally to something fun.

Try not to consider what can turn out badly, yet what can go right-As a rule, overthinking is brought about by a solitary feeling: dread. When you center around all the negative things that may occur, it is anything but difficult to end up deadened. If you feel that you might be going down this road for any reason, then stop yourself. Picture every one of the things that can go right and keep those contemplations present and in advance.

Nobody can foresee the future; the total of what we have is present. If you spend the current minute stressing over the future, you deny yourself of your time now. Investing energy, later on, is just not beneficial. Invest that energy instead on things that give you satisfaction.

For us all who are hanging tight for flawlessness, we can quit holding up this moment. Being driven is incredible, yet going for flawlessness is ridiculous, illogical, and crippling. The minute you begin thinking, "This should be immaculate" is simply the minute you have to remind yourself, "Sitting tight for impeccable is never as brilliant as gaining ground."

Life consists of thousands of moments, but we only live one moment at a time. When we start changing this moment, we start changing our lives. Are you somebody who likes to overthink things? Trinidad Hunt. Nonetheless, what exactly is over-thinking? According to psychologists, who have done extensive research in the field, rethinking is' too much, needlessly and passively thinking; always pondering the significance, triggers and conse-quences of your personality, your emotions and particularly your problems.' It can mean lying awake at night thinking, "This economy is terrible; my savings are not worth it; I will probably lose my job and, I will never be able to send my kids back to college." Or it can mean thinking about how unat-tractive your delicate and wispy hair is several times over the day. Three days ago. Is he mad about some-thing? Is he punishing me? Am I too insignificant to bother?" Someone who spends a lot of time wondering why a friend or boss hasn't made eye contact or spoken to them in a room, sits down to feel bad and then doesn't think it's worth putting in the effort or taking risks involved in top performance. Most people believe that if they feel disappointed or depressed by certain things, it will encourage them to think deeply and examine the situation to sort it out. When we look at science, the truth is just the opposite. Instead of being supportive, constant ruminations about possible adverse incidents tend to make people worse. Yes, according to Lyubomirsky, there is widespread and significant evidence that thinking about a painful or troubling situation is terrible for us over and over (also called "rumination"). It can be so harmful that it prevents us from taking significant proactive steps to improve the condition and can lead to an increasing deterioration of attitude, cynical distortion of reality, and even clinical depression in those who are vulnerable. Life and the world around you are all full of problems, from minor annoyances, mistakes, and imperfections to major tragic events and frightening threats and possibilities. It does not make us more stable or somehow less vulnerable to any of these innovations. It makes us feel worse and makes us less likely to take constructive action to improve our attitude or to reverse those changes. How can your job, your personal goals, your family, and your relationships be overlooked? It can make you feel so pessimistic that you avoid taking risks, reaching out to others, and making significant efforts to be successful. It can make it hard and even frustrating to be around for those who most matter to you. Ultimately, rethinking, with its forecasts of inevitable failure and terrible consequences, can drain the optimism required to work hard, speak up, and spread good thoughts.

Revisiting your daily objectives holds a lot of weight in today's society, where people flounder and don't know what they truly want. Instead, they struggle to make ends meet, have to plan to get themselves out of sticky situations and find themselves more lost than ever. You might be buried in your to-do list and don't know how to get out of it. The best approach is to stick to your goals.

Immediately when you get up in the morning, write down your daily goals, as well as the tasks and activities you hope to accomplish in your future. You will become motivated to do all the things you set out to do, and then you will be sure of a better future.

You might be thinking, "Where am I going to be in five or ten years?" To answer this vital question, you need to examine what you are doing at this moment. How are you tackling your goals daily? How are you growing or learning? Are you approaching your goals from a progressive and positive perspective?

Many people think that events are going to shift

their future in the direction where they want to go. They mystically believe that some miracle is going to make their dreams come true. However, this is not a reality. Instead, your life will shift in new directions only when you decide you want to alter it. How are you acting to ensure that you can get out of your unpleasant circumstances? You have to consider all the implications of your daily actions.

Sometimes, you have to look forward and then look backward. Use the future anterior tense in this case. After I achieve my dreams, I will have done _____ every day. For example, I will have worked out more, read more, and gotten a lot of tasks done.

Think as though you have already achieved your dreams and then work backward. You will then find that success is around the corner.

Hard times are sure to strike you, and you have to be ready for them. You need to be proactive in the process. Don't let it catch you by surprise. You must have a plan in place that you will turn to if and when you go through trials and tribulations. As you write out your goals, you need to stick to them in every situation. When you encounter the rocks on life's path, you need to know precisely how you will respond.

4

STOP YOUR THOUGHTS IN THE MOMENT AND PRACTICE BEING PRESENT

*M*ost people suffering from chronic stress, anxiety, and panic disorders develop an unhealthy habit, which makes them feel more anxious, less comfortable, and less satisfied. For some, their unhealthy habits – small exercise, irregular sleep, running food – had been in play long before the anxiety disorder developed, and perhaps one of the reasons why they were first out of touch with anxiety. For others, their unhealthy habits started as they grew anxiety issues. You skipped the workout because you were too afraid and afraid to have a quick walk or a morning run into your day. They often eat on the run or eat fat and sugar when they are anxious or down. They have fast food. Whether your dysfunctional patterns have come before or after your nervous problems, you need to fix these unhealthy environments.

You can learn in this chapter about the vital part of the management of your anxiety and the full recovery from your excessive anxiety and anxiety disorder by exercise, and sleep.

How Regular Exercise, Good Nutrition, And Adequate Sleep Can Help.

You may have problems doing the things you know may help if you are having excessive anxiety or an anxiety disorder. If you take 30 minutes to walk around the block, you can interrupt your workout exercises, because you too are upset that an important deadline is missed. You can save lunch and eat junk food at your office because in the morning you were too busy packing lunch. And what's the difference? You don't know anyway what you drank because you didn't eat attentively. You can remain exhausted as you try to fit another thing in your day, then lie awake thinking that because of tiredness and poor sleep, you might no longer be your best the next day. Yet regular exercise, proper nutrition, and good sleep are vital elements of any scheme that can fully recover from chronic stress and anxiety disorder.

You'll better protect yourself from stress and experience fewer symptoms of too much anxiety through regular exercise. Exercise can not only reduce the strength of your stress response over time, but you will also feel less nervous for some time after exercising every day. You can shield yourself from unnecessary spikes of blood sugar levels with proper nutrition, which can increase your depression and worsen your mood. Adequate nutrition also removes your depression aggravating compounds such as caffeine, which can relax the body and spirit, or even boost your health, in your diet. You will protect yourself from fluctuations in your anxious reaction and mood, if you're not well-rested, with sufficient sleep. They will also look out against the extra stress and worry that many people begin to think about and worry about the consequences of rest.

GETTING AND STAYING IN SHAPE

Daily exercise is good for almost everybody, but it is particularly crucial if you have an anxiety disorder. Several studies have shown that people with regular exercise have fewer effects of anxiety and depression and lower rates. Also, the practice seems to protect people against anxiety and mood conditions. Regular exercise has another advantage. After your workout, you will feel less anxious and feel more comfortable.

In other words, although it may take weeks for you to feel less nervous about doing this significantly, you will not feel more anxious after the workout, and each day you get this advantage. In reality, the more you are involved, the more so are the immediate effects of exercise.

Your willingness to do this will affect how you practice and what amount and type of exercise you choose. Here are a few tips to help you develop an exercise routine that you will not only love but also like to do regularly.

Fit an exercise routine into your life instead of fitting your life into an exercise routine. They do the best practice-regularly. In other words, regular people have chosen a workout routine that works for them in their lives. When you know, for example, that swimming would be right for you, but it is challenging to do a tour of the pool (the journey back and forth, the bathing, the shower). So as long as you believe you "can" dive, swimming in some other way might make more sense. Maybe it's better to just walk out of the door to stretch or jog around, or you can go and get out of work by car. For example, you can swim if you can concentrate on it, but it may be a mistake to build an exercise schedule around an unusual activity. Therefore, when you face the pressure of turning your current life into one particular practice, you can enjoy the event less.

Enjoy yourself. Regardless of how you prefer to exercise, you will have less fun some days than other days. If you go, you will one day feel like pushing a fridge down the sidewalk, and you must drive to complete the race. You will have a glorious time on other days. You'll be the same size, but you'll feel lighter and faster, and you will have an incredible sense of well-being. So running is a beautiful thing – shift your arms and legs, balance, let your body do what it's meant to do minute by minute. Nevertheless, even in days where the workout schedule is not especially enjoyed, you will still enjoy the training itself; after and after exercise, you will feel less stressed. It can help you remember when you roll the cooler down the sidewalk behind you.

If you pick a kind of workout you like: tennis, running, and salsa dancing, you will enjoy exercising more. Exercise does not mean to run a mile or to swim for 50 laps before work. When it suits your skills and interests, aerobic training can be enjoyable. You can do any physical activity that your heart pumps. You might want to choose three or five things that you may want to keep your exercise healthy and fun if you never enjoyed it. Then decide when you

can participate in these things on your daily schedule. Be as rational as you can. A 30-minute walk in
the countryside after school, when you have to get
your child to tutor or make a family dinner, can be
hard for your day; shooting your child in the court-
yard with hoops for 30 minutes after tutoring, but it
could be suitable for your day before lunch.

Reward yourself. There is an excellent reward
for the immediate benefits of running–reduced
depression and more well-being. Track your workout
routine and use this immediate advantage to repay
you, including the decline in your stress response
after training. You can also track the workout
routine's enjoyment.

Find other ways to make a difference while exercising. Take a warm shower after the exercise for a
few minutes. Good job, say to yourself; believe it.
Smile, after use, Any work is a good job. Note, after
some days of exercising, you will feel great, and not
so big some days. Award yourself. Use the reward
plan of dot-to-dot. Draw an image that is an excellent
reward using a sheet of graph paper and draw it.
Click on a picture of your new phone or on a palm
tree for that weekend, for example, to make a picture
from a magazine. Put the cut-out image on the paper
graph and trace it slightly. Now draw a dot where

the image touches a line on the paper. Whenever you exercise, darken one point and connect with the one that you just darkened to the previous darkened dot. Take a small bonus per third or fourth point you obscure; a manicure, a movie, an hour to do correctly, and just what you want to. When you attach all the points, award yourself the big prize.

Develop the habit of exercising. There are major customary things, like "thank you" if someone does something good for you or gives you a free ride to work in the morning even when you want to go to the beach. Yet customs can also cause problems. Take into account the anxious patterns or habits in your fearful response. How useful are these customs? Developing an exercise habit will assist you in changing the harmless habits and trends in your anxious reaction. A definite pattern of exercise may increase the flexibility and emotional response to objects, activities, and situations of your thinking and actions. But they can be as hard to construct as they can break, as can many habits. Try to follow R four: Routine, Reward, Remind, and Relax to create a practice habit.

Do you think about where your life is headed now? Do you plan for the future only to see your plans turn to nothing? You're not alone. Self-discipline is a tireless effort, and it does not come easy to most people. Have you ever made a promise to yourself on New Year's Eve that you won't smoke another cigarette or have another drink, only to see your resolution come under fire the next day? We all find ourselves struggling to make and keep our New Year's resolutions because we simply don't have the self-discipline and willpower necessary to keep these promises to ourselves.

Because it is hard to keep our resolutions, we should consider the different ways we can make self-discipline last in our lives. There are a variety of ways we can limit our consumption of sugar, cut down on cigarettes, eliminate excessive binge-watching of TV and movies, etc. Let's look at some ways you can stop procrastinating on building self-discipline and start fresh today.

What we need to recognize is that the power lies within ourselves to change things. We should take full responsibility for our actions and do the things that will get us on the entire road to recovery. Recognize that no one is going to make you successful in your life. Only you can do this for yourself. You should be fully responsible for your finances, happiness, success, and health. Once you leave behind the influences of family, including relying on mom and dad or other people in your life and begin to make choices for yourself, you become fully responsible for what happens in your life and your preferences.

It is you who chooses the job you work at, the people you live with, your significant other, and how much you work out every day. You have to decide to use your time wisely. The decisions you make every day will have temporary and long-term consequences.

To improve your quality of life, you should become an expert in decision-making. Don't blame other people for your poor decision. It makes you look weak and irresponsible. Take responsibility for all the choices you make in your life. Although you may not be in control of all situations, you can control how you will respond: either maturely or foolishly.

Brian Tracy has talked about the fact that the biggest hindrance to a person's success is the easy way out. By choosing things that are easy for you, it will become impossible to achieve success and breakthroughs in the areas of your life that you want to change. Every battle we fight requires us to sacrifice something, and every success we can have has to have something that we give. However, most people never do this because they are lazy and unmotivated.

If you avoid doing the necessary things, you will avoid growing as a person, and you will also lose a sense of self-confidence. When you project yourself in a negative light, your reputation will paint you as a lazy and pitiful person.

If you want to achieve self-discipline, it will require a vision of where you want to be, a game plan, and repeated patterns that continue to work. It will be simple to write up your goals and determine what steps you need to take. But the last part is going to be the hardest because it requires your entire industry to achieve.

Do the things that are necessary and difficult because those things are going to matter more than the easy and fun aspects of life. You sometimes have to bust your butt to get ahead, and this is a crucial step to take. For you to achieve a high level of self-discipline, you should bear in mind that there is a bigger picture out there. You have to recall the reasoning for your actions and keep your promises, although the going will become tough. Bear in mind. However, that hard work does not have to be futile, like Sisyphus rolling the stone up the hill. But with your objectives in mind, you will be able to fulfill your goals.

By making a contract with yourself, you will

ensure that you don't break it, and you can make it a reality. Although you might not be able to achieve your goal immediately, it will happen eventually.

Because nothing in life is going to be simple, you must sacrifice your sleep, time, and effort to achieve the things you want. Undoubtedly, you will encounter situations that will set you back. As you edge closer to your success, you will also meet more adversity and testing than before. But as you pass each life test, you will find that your resolve becomes more firm and secure. Moreover, you become more resilient and bulletproof. Think of all the arrows coming out at you, but you're able to dodge them and become more influential in the process. Your shield of honor and motivation will be what get you through the difficult times.

Success has to be hard because it makes you stand out from the crowd. If it were easy, anyone could accomplish it, and then it wouldn't exist. It would be the easy road that leads to destruction. However, success is a road that you need to take, and it is the narrow way that not everyone is going to be able to achieve. The majority of people will fail to see it materialize.

Many people surrender to their fear and anxiety before they achieve their goals. They cross a mile-marker, and then they need to push themselves to run the race or the marathon, only to have their hope dashed by an obstacle that comes their way.

The moral of the story is that you need never to give up. Don't give in to the fear that may crush you. Instead, face your fear and own up to the fact that life is hard. Face everything with a mindset that you can do it because you're worth it.

Practice gratitude, and make it a daily habit. It is one of the secrets of highly successful people; they have made practicing gratitude a part of their daily habits. It is an effortless task, and it entails that you notice every last good thing that happens to you every day. When you are done seeing the little details and the God things that have happened to you that day, write them down in a journal. This practice may be hard to keep up at first, but the aim is to get you to a place where you develop the eye that has been trained to see the right things and a reason to be grateful in every situation.

Whenever you are about to be overwhelmed by negative thoughts and the reality of the fact that life can be harmful, commit to fixating on thinking good thoughts. There has to be a silver lining to hold on to amid every storm, right? That is the same thing you do once you carry out this exercise. Every time you are about to be overwhelmed by something negative, pick out memory from your past and fixate on it. Let it be a memory that puts a smile on your face. Doing this will make sure that you are not overwhelmed by the feelings of weakness that come with thinking of negativity all the time.

Talk to someone. Sometimes, it may not be easy for you to achieve this all by yourself, and that is why it becomes vital for you to talk to someone. It may be a therapist or a trusted person who can help you out of the dark place, but the goal is to make sure that you do not sink into the pool of feeling bad when you can reach out to someone who can offer some sort of help to you. The result of this is that they hardly ever get to live in the present, and if you do not live in the present, then you do not have any hopes of achieving anything remarkable.

Goal-oriented people know that if they must achieve the things that they have set out to make, they owe it to themselves and to the people around them to live in the moment. They know this because they have been in the place where they stressed out about everything that was not the present, and they were able to tell after a long time that all they did was just waste their time. Here are a few reasons why you must live in the present.

Have this knowledge and be very clear about it; the past is in the past for a reason. There is nothing you can do to change it, and the only definite way to take a look at your history is to try and draw lessons from it that you can apply to the present to change the future.

For example, a man who has just been relieved of his job can choose to sit down all day and lament the fact that he was sacked, or he can decide to take a look at his contribution to the whole thing. It could have been that he was not as productive as he should have been, or that there were other reasons why he was relieved. In place of crying incessantly about the job he lost, he can take it upon himself to improve his skill set so that he can become an employable worker in another firm, and be more productive at his new job. It is the mindset you must adopt if you are going to start living in the present.

There are times it helps for you to get off your mind from the big goal and focus on the small wins that will get you to your big goal. Let's face it; it is a great thing to feel that rush of dopamine and feel happy at the thoughts that you have a big goal to meet. However, it can be daunting just to keep an eye on the target. So instead of looking at the big goal and getting discouraged at how impossible it seems, focus more on the little wins that will culminate in the big goal. Instead of stressing out about how far your Ph.D. appears to be from you, focus on acing all your courses in all your exams, and you would be surprised at how fast you will end up getting to the big goal you have set for yourself.

Understand that even the best of plans is not that foolproof. One of the reasons why you never get much done is the fact that you spend a lot of time planning and analyzing how you will have the perfect thing happen for you. While it is excellent to be meticulous, it is worthy to note that even the best and most detailed plans are still not immune to suffering from a few unforeseen circumstances. This knowledge will make you know that the best thing to do is to live in the now and take the days as they show up. Things do not always happen as you would want them to, and you should have this in mind as you walk through your everyday life.

5

TAKE CONTROL OF YOUR EMOTIONS

*L*isten to Yourself; this takes us back to the importance of positive self-talk. To tame your thoughts, start by listening to yourself. Do this as though you were explaining something to other people. How would you want to tell other people about the story of your life? Without a doubt, you would want to talk about everything that you have done well. No one would want to tell others negative stories about themselves. Therefore, you should adopt a similar attitude when listening to yourself. Focus on treating yourself with the same respect that you would expect from other people. It means that you should strive to focus on thoughts that put yourself in a positive light. Your Inner Self is Listening; you should always bear in mind that your inner self is listening to your thoughts; this is the emotional you. So, if you continue thinking about negative things, your inner self will look and conform to how you expect it to behave. When thinking positively, it will also listen to you and adapt to help you perceive life with optimism. Therefore, before blaming other people for the bad things that are happening to you, remember that there is someone within you who is listening to your self-talk.

Befriend Your Emotional Guidance System. There are many cues that you can grasp from your emotions. Learning how to tame your mind can be effectively achieved by being mindful of your feelings. These emotions can quickly tell you when you are angry or feeling anxious or overwhelmed about something. Therefore, by being aware of your beliefs, you can master control over your mind before turning to think about all the negative things. The point here is that you should pause every time you notice that your emotions have changed. You should take some time to evaluate your feelings and the ensuing thoughts before they gain momentum. The effect of this is that it will help you develop an attitude of thinking twice before doing anything. Before doing anything, you will reflect on whether what you're about to do is favorable or not. You increase the likelihood of making the right decisions without allowing emotions to cloud your judgment.

Another practical tip that can make a difference in how you think is visualizing stop signs that signal to you that you should stop thinking about something. Your stop signs will warrant that you can regain your senses and avoid thinking about your past or worrying about your future. The best way of using these stop signs is to remind you that your thoughts are not helping to build you up. For instance, you can come up with a stop sign that tells you that you are overthinking about events that prevent you from being happy. It might take some time for you to master how to use these stop signs, but the outcome will be rewarding as it will enhance your self-awareness. When thinking about improving our health, we know perfectly well that this can only be done by eating right. The foods that you choose to eat have an impact on your health. In the same manner, the words that float around in your mind affect your mental health. It means that it is essential that you control the information that you feed into your mind. For example, watching horrific content on television might not be as entertaining as you think. In the long run, this will harm how you feel and the thoughts that frequent your mind.

Becoming the master of your mind also demands that you stay on top of your game. You have to keep yourself engaged in positive gear. Sure, there are instances when you might slip up and think negatively, but with the right affirmations, you will feel unstoppable. Have these affirmations in areas where you can easily see them. Pin them next to your files in your office. Before going to bed, remind yourself of your higher purpose by reading out these affirmations to yourself. They can eliminate anxiety and soothe you to sleep better. Increasing your self-awareness about your thoughts will give you the advantage of identifying unnecessary thoughts and emotions. When you do this consistently, you will find it easier to declutter your mind. The notion of taking out the trash shouldn't drive you to overthink about your past. Instead, the point here is to develop an attitude where you simply admit that some thoughts are not worth holding. Practice meditation exercises as a way of increasing your self-awareness. It is the best way of raising your antennas high enough to pick any signals of unwanted thoughts in your mind.

There is a good reason why you should strive to be happy. Most people have never realized that there are adverse effects of focusing too much on trying for positivity. Sure, we all want our lives to be full of happiness. However, we should come to terms with the fact that too much of anything is detrimental. It also applies to satisfaction. When we go about chasing happiness, we surround ourselves with all the things that can keep us entertained and full of joy. The downside of this kind of life is that it can blind us with unrealistic optimism.

Indeed, without going through pain in life, it is challenging to grow. You will not learn how to deal with the challenges of life that transform you into a healthy human being. Therefore, this should signal to you that going through anxiety and stress in the short run is not a bad thing. It is healthy. There are two forms of happiness: eudaimonic and hedonic joy. You should learn to recognize the kind of pleasure that you are chasing in your life. Hedonistic happiness is the type of fun that brings enjoyment and satisfaction. Therefore, if you are seeking hedonistic happiness in your life, it means that your main goal in life is to find pleasure. To these individuals, being happy involves merely doing things they enjoy and seek things that make them feel good.

On the other hand, eudaimonic happiness refers to the type of contentment, where satisfaction is not the primary goal in life. In this case, people pursue things of value in their lives that could lead to true happiness. The striking difference in the two forms of happiness is that eudaimonic happiness creates happiness as a by-product of the things that you focus on. Conversely, hedonic happiness only focuses on pleasure as a motivational factor. The beauty behind eudaimonic happiness is that it creates a fulfilling form of joy in the long haul. Concerning the notion of taming your thoughts, you should embrace the idea of chasing the eudaimonic kind of happiness. Don't just strive to be happy by seeking worldly pleasures. Focus more on what adds value to your life, and you will feel more satisfied in the long run.

There is nothing wrong with expressing your authentic emotions. Unfortunately, society castigates people that show their real feelings and celebrates those that bottle up emotions in a misguided effort to create a standardized culture. Human behavior is dynamic, and it cannot be regulated, but we can build a shared spectrum of what is ideal and what is not. Against this understanding, do not blame yourself as being a mess or easily irked because it is the society that is pushing for suppressing authentic feelings. However, you must find a safe way to defuse negative emotions to avoid creating   fear   and   avoidance   from   people around you.

"Maintain calmness even when you have a thousand reasons not to be" Even though this quote seems to contradict the first quote, it is not. While it is vital to manifest your emotions, both positive and negative, it is essential to take time before fully expressing negative emotions. For positive emotions, it might be excusable to act impulsively, but it is still advisable to exercise restraint. Remember that within the context of emotional intelligence, it is critical to consider how others feel. Your excitement could be happening at a time when one of your colleagues has been sacked or going through a divorce. With this understanding, learning to slow down your reaction can help improve your emotional intelligence. Emotions are impulsive, and you will have to learn to anticipate certain emotions to enhance the manner that you react to them.

"Emotional health affects your self-esteem" you must learn to diagnose yourself because your emotional state affects your self-esteem levels. By identifying what troubling you is, it will enable you to read more about the trigger and how to handle it before it fully manifests. For emphasis, most individuals tend to overlook the fact that positive emotions can also adversely impact your personality. For instance, if you are highly excitable, there are chances that you are likely to overlook finer details of anything and may have difficulties planning for the long-term. In other terms, excessively manifesting positive emotions can make you highly vulnerable to environmental factors, as any significant change may make it difficult for you to recover.

Equally important is that part of your self-esteem constitutes the self-assurance that you can navigate any situation. For this reason, you must experience or become aware of both negative and positive emotions. As expected, building the ability to recognize your emotional health and attend to it happens over time with guidance and commitment. Once you master the art of diagnosing and fixing your emotional health, then your levels of self-esteem will increase, as you are likely to navigate any situation. Simply put, adverse emotional health will lower your self-esteem levels. One of the ways of diagnosing yourself is through meditation and learning to extricate yourself from your thoughts to develop an independent view of the situation.

"Life is an active process" Through acknowledging that life is an active process, you recognize that human behavior and actions are dynamic.

Human behavior is both predictable and uncertain. What differentiates an emotionally stable person from a highly sensitive individual is their emotional intelligence levels. Individuals regarded as emotionally permanent exhibit the desired ability to express both negative and positive emotions acceptably through training or experience. The emphasis is on the degree of reacting to emotions and that all emotions should be shown. Locking up emotions is counterproductive as, at one point, you will experience an emotional outburst or get overwhelmed by the feelings and make an irrational and sometimes fatal decision. You should remember that bottling up emotions could be a danger not only to you but to those around, including physical systems, if you work in critical installations.

Since life is an active process, you should accept that learning would not stop. There will be new techniques and suggestions that are new to you, and it will require mentorship and training to master them. All these realizations encourage us to try learning about emotional intelligence since life is an active process, and there are high chances of improving our emotional intelligence. From the feedback you gather about the way you react to particular situations, you should seek ways to acknowledge and manage the specific reaction. Adjusting your emotional intelligence level to desirable levels are informed by the fact the human mind and emotional state can be altered. These realizations are the core pillars of advancing emotional intelligence as a concept to be learned, internalized, and operationalized.

For example, remember when you used to cry when left alone as a child, but as you grew up, you started cherishing freedom. As a toddler, your mind and exposure had only assured you that you could only be safe around your parents or caregiver. The extrication of the caregiver from your life temporarily generated uncertainty and unfamiliarity. You expressed the negative emotions by crying continuously. However, as you grew, you learned to convert the absence of caregivers in your life temporarily as an opportunity to explore yourself and your environment. The temporary freedom granted you a chance to express positive emotions in the form of feeling energized, playful, and confident. What we learn from this simple illustration is that life is an active process, and we express certain emotions based on our understanding of our self and the immediate environment. Emotional intelligence can be learned by manipulating the internal and external factors that make us react in a specific manner.

"Through enlarging the acknowledgment spectrum, your emotional intelligence begins to grow."

Through this statement, we learned that loosening up and being open-minded up can lessen the need to bottle up emotions as well as increasing chances of manifesting negative emotions. As indicated earlier, stereotypes and other prejudices predispose you to make premature judgments that compromise empathy in interactions. Furthermore, sustaining prejudices requires significant mental while denying you numerous opportunities to recognize positive emotions. At an individual level, lack of being open-minded may use up your physical and mental energy as you try to force a conclusion where it should not suffice. Therefore, learning to allow a significant degree of freedom before concluding allows you more options, some of which are likely to lead to a decreased need to manifest negative emotions.

Additionally, being open-minded increases empathy quality in conversations. Think of trying to have a conversation with a divorcee as having performed an opinion that divorcees entered a marriage institution before adequately courting.

While having an interview with the divorcee, your mind will always extrapolate your views from the premise that divorcees come to a marriage union before sufficiently knowing each other well. In essence, you are not actively listening to the individual you are talking to because you have allowed the little knowledge you have to become the ultimate knowledge. Some educationists argue that the most overlooked aspect of learning is the ability to unlearn, which most people struggle with.

"Meditation is not necessarily emotional intelligence, but it can be a critical tool for emotional intelligence" Even though meditation has numerous benefits, it is not necessarily emotional intelligence. The importance of meditation is that it can significantly increase the self-awareness of an individual. As seen earlier, self-awareness is a critical plank of emotional intelligence. Without individual learning to understand itself and its shortcomings, there is little motivation to seek help and commit to the advice and training provided after that. In the initial stages of improving an individual's emotional intelligence, meditation is a valuable tool. Meditation can be a form of self-feedback, and it can also be used as a means for an individual to remove himself from the self to form an alternate view of everything.

However, if a person is not eased with meditation, the person should not be forced to undertake it.

"Develop healthy boundaries and enforce them" While a lot has been presented on how to be considerate of others and how to adjust your desires to attain balance with others, there is a need for setting boundaries. You can still specify and enforce limits of what you can absorb and what you can manifest. Remember that while adjusting yourself to listen and empathize with others, they also have a moral duty to understand and accept you. Sometimes not all people will easily read your limits, and for this reason, it is essential that you explicitly define the boundaries you can go and the limits that they are allowed to reach when dealing with you.

Even though it appears a manageable undertaking, most individuals set limits but lack the spine to enforce such boundaries. Allowing other peoples to overstep and violate your restrictions will reverse all gains you have made in developing emotional intelligence. While pursuing the definition of limits allowable, it is essential to be considerate and respectful of yourself and others. There is a difference between letting people know the limits eligible and imposing their restrictions on them. For this reason, effective communication is inherent in emotional intelligence.

Remember, negative emotions such as anger can be enhanced by failing to let others know of the allowable limits. Fortunately, like any other aspect of emotional intelligence, you can learn how to say no respectfully and firmly.

"Anger is not a weakness; it is an emotion, but the manner of handling it can be a weakness."

If you accept that emotions are a form of energy, then you will realize why it is essential to express them because, in this way, you will dissipate the heat and attain equilibrium. We correctly argued that locking up emotions is counterproductive as, at one point, you will experience an emotional outburst, or you will act irrationally endangering yourself, others, and the systems around you. Anger is a common negative emotion that many wrongly assume that it should be suppressed. In this book, we are arguing that violence should be expressed as an emotion. Still, it should be shown when it is building up in various ways of managing anger, such as breathing deep or counting up to one hundred before making a decision when angry.

"Sometimes spiritualism and culture can enhance or worsen emotional intelligence" There are some religious practices that infuse aspects of meditation that can help an individual attain self-awareness. By understanding yourself, your strengths, and your weaknesses, you will begin the journey of improving your emotional intelligence levels. For instance, saying a prayer may allow a person to engage in constructive soliloquy, which enables the individual to express his or her feelings instead of locking them up. On the other hand, some cultural practices may contribute to increasing emotional intelligence. For instance, Western cultures may encourage expressing of emotions while most African cultures demand that men bottle up feelings. However, it is essential to remember that cultural influence is significant to the environmental factors that may favor being expressive or reserved.

Expectedly, spiritualism and culture can also worsen the emotional intelligence levels of a person. For instance, religious practice that qualifies negative feelings as expected norms that one should live with can aggravate poor emotional reactions to challenging situations. Individuals subscribing to such methods may not see the need to seek help as such emotions are qualified as expected, and one should instead toughen up. Some cultures frown at the thought of men exhibiting emotions, especially negative emotions forcing such individuals to feel ashamed of being emotional beings. When you analyze the contribution of your spirituality and cultural influences to your emotional intelligence levels, you will pick what positively contributes to your emotional intelligence and drop others that aggravate the inappropriate handling of feelings.

"Avoid excuses as they equate to running away from reality" At one point in life, each one of us may have resorted to excuses because they provided an effective way to avoid protracted conversation that might be difficult. Unfortunately, reasons are merely a cover of underlying issues and do not offer any real solution. You must learn to face your emotions and their impact rather than justifying why you behaved in the manner that you did. Emotional intelligence offers a long-term approach to meeting your fears and joys individually and in the public sphere. Excuses work against the spirit of emotional intelligence, as they are technically lies while passionate intelligence advocates for honesty and consideration of all parties involved in an interaction.

While human behavior is dynamic and unpredictable, emotional intelligence is highly predictable. Emotional intelligence can be seen as a universal template for expressing and managing each emotional reaction. This quality of emotional intelligence makes learning and applying emotional intelligence impressive as you can develop a custom approach to your emotions that applies to nearly all of your situations. As indicated, negative feelings and positive emotions are almost finite even though how we react varies. The variation to the way each person responds to emotions varies, but the typical reactions are reasonably predictable. All these attributes make emotional intelligence highly learnable and applicable by all persons. When you start exploring emotional intelligence to improve your personality and character, remember that you do not have to learn everything in a day, month, or year. Start by analyzing your strengths and shortcomings and focus first on your weaknesses. It is advisable to learn bit by bit according to your synthesis and application. With time, you can explore the entire spectrum of emotional intelligence, including the areas that touch on your strengths. By accepting that there are several layers of emotional intelligence, you will focus on what you need and move on to the next when you have the confidence that you have gained much from the current level.

6

REALIZE THAT YOU CANNOT
CONTROL EVERYTHING

*T*here are different ways of defining a simple life. What a simple life is to you can mean a different thing to another person. However, the best way of describing a simple life is by understanding that it centers around the idea of getting rid of what you deem unessential in your life. In other words, it means spending most of your time doing what you value the most. A simple life means avoiding wasting your valuable time on things that are not important. As such, you value-creating time for people and experiences that add meaning to your life. Concerning clutter, it means freeing your mind from potential distractions that could prevent you from thinking straight and enjoying life.

Living a simple life is not as simple as it sounds. It's something that calls for patience simply because it's a journey and not a destination. The easiest way to understand how to live a simple life is by identifying the things that are important to you and eliminating everything else. To simplify your life Start by identifying what you value most in your life. Make a list of these things. While doing this, you must limit this list to 4 or 5 items. The importance of defining your list to a few words is that it creates room for essential things in your life that may arise later. As a result, attending to the first will create a more fulfilling feeling than just approaching life randomly.

It is also crucial that you evaluate how you spend your time. Monitor how you use your time from the time you wake up to the end of the day. Create a list of the things that you often prioritize and those that usually distract you. By doing this frequently, you will identify things that only consume time and that are not important to you. In other words, you can redesign your day and work productively towards achieving your daily goals.

A fundamental habit that you ought to develop as you try to simplify your life is to learn to say no.

Indeed, it is never easy to say no to your friends and colleagues at work. Unfortunately, this creates a situation where your to-do list will always be packed. What you should understand is that other people will be completing their tasks because you are helping them do what needs to be done on their to-do lists. On your end, you will have a lot of pending. It is because you chose to accept extra tasks without putting yourself first. Therefore, it's never a bad thing to say no when you are doing it for the right reasons.

With the advancement in technology, you can access information at the touch of a button. From a positive perspective, this makes it easy for us to communicate with our loved ones and our friends. Social media has changed the way people and businesses communicate. People should realize that too much media consumption can harm us. It pollutes our minds by altering the perceptions that we already have about life. We end up developing new ways of living our lives based on the opinions that we have recently emerged. Unfortunately, this is how we complicate our lives.

Simplifying your life also demands that you declutter the physical space around you. It is easy to work in a tidy area compared to a room filled with clutter. Clutter prevents you from thinking straight. Before getting rid of clutter in your mind as earlier recommended, start by decluttering the space around you. Get rid of things in your house that don't add value to you. Usually, we hold on to something without realizing that they are only taking away space for more important things. From your bedroom to your kitchen, you should work on decluttering your space. Ideally, the physical space that you create will also have a positive impact on how you think and make decisions.

Once you eliminate unimportant things in your life, you will have more time to focus on other essential items. Therefore, use this time wisely by doing what you love. Remember the list of crucial things that you created? Use this extra time to work on these things. Eventually, you will live a simple yet fulfilling life. It will be daunting to live a simple life when toxic people surround you. These are people who never seem to add value to your life in any way. The worst thing is that they drain energy from you as they always think negatively. Also, they are the people that push you around to help them without stopping to help you. Sure, some of these individuals are your best friends because there is a lot that you have been through with them. However, a keen eye on your relationship with them will reveal the fact that there is nothing you benefit from being friends with them. So, the best thing you can and should do is to eliminate them from your life. It might sound harsh. But, the reality is that you will be doing yourself a favor by opening doors for more fruitful relationships.

Living a simple life also means that you should plan what you eat. Eating is part of your daily routine. It is something that you do throughout the day as long as you feel hungry. Accordingly, planning for your meals shouldn't be neglected. Make it a priority on your to-do list. Don't waste your time every day trying to figure out what you will be having for lunch or dinner. Just plan it. The good news is that doing this increases the likelihood of eating healthy foods that contribute to a productive lifestyle. Frequently, people choose to ignore the debts that they have with the hopes that it will help them stop worrying. It doesn't help since you will only procrastinate the decision to pay your debts. Come up with a plan of how you will pay off your debts. Financially, it will help you make better decisions and open doors for business opportunities.

A simple life doesn't have to be something that is

beyond your reach. It's all about identifying the things that are of great importance to you and prioritizing them. It creates time for you to enjoy with family and friends. If everyone in the world made a list of the points and traits they think about when they think about their view of themselves, you would most likely see a lot of repeated essential factors. The mistakes, triumphs, accidents, and successes that come throughout life all carry their emotional and psychological influences with them. It's these influences that are most powerful when it comes to shaping how a person views themselves and their current lifestyle or life situation. The more positive impacts and experiences a person can collect, the better their self-esteem will be, and the more emotionally in control they will find themselves when stressful situations arise.

Confidence (particularly when described as self-confidence) refers to faith a person has in their knowledge, experience, skills, and abilities. Depending on how much belief someone has in the things they know, the things they say, and the things they do during their personal or professional interactions, the higher a person's confidence levels will be.

A person's confidence comes from their opinion

of and trust in their strengths and abilities. This trust and faith most often are the result of positive experiences such as promotions at work or awards at school. The more experience they have and proof they have been able to collect that they know or what they are talking about, then the higher their self-confidence will be, and the more that will start to affect other areas of their life positively.

Many people have a high level of self-esteem. Still, they find that they lack confidence, especially in certain situations like when asked to do something without time to prepare, but are concerned with how others will react to it. Hence, they decide just to keep their hand down.

As different as they can be, there are also plenty of situations and experiences that can be caused by interconnected levels of self-esteem and confidence. The more understanding, experienced, and control a person has over their self-esteem and confidence levels, the better off they will be in all opportunities they attempt or goals they strive for throughout their life.

Strengthening these traits not only helps with improving a person's overall mental, psychological, and emotional health, but it also comes with a variety of other benefits that can help improve someone's health and wellness in a wide range of styles. Here is a look at some of the most popular and widely reported benefits people have experienced in their quests for higher self-esteem and confidence!

Those with higher self-esteem and personal confidence are less likely to be people pleasers or develop people-pleasing habits than those with lower opinions of themselves or their abilities.

They also tend to have better performance ratings and higher success rates in leadership roles.

Not only are they more personable with customers or other audiences, but they are also more empathetic with employers or co-workers and better able to boost morale during times of high demand or increased stress levels.

They are also more likely to have higher success rates with setting and reaching personal and professional goals because they are more self-aware of their mental, psychological, emotional changes, and how it affects their daily performance.

Those with higher self-esteem and confidence levels report more personal and professional satisfaction throughout their lives. They are more likely to take up opportunities when offered.

One of the biggest problems with overthinking is

that it leads to procrastination. The whole point of the brain for causing anxiety is to push you into inactivity. It wants you to stick to a corner so that the risk can be minimized. Procrastination is one of the most common side-effects of overthinking. It keeps you in a never-ending loop of thinking that has no scope of action. Your mind can keep forming strategies and then discarding them after a point to create newer and better ones.

What you need is a plan to break the chain of thoughts and get into action. The longer you keep thinking, the harder it will get to stop overthinking about it. Procrastination can be one of the most significant negative traits of an overthinking person, and it would also support your habit of not taking action on time.

Given below are five strategies that can help you in ditching the thinking mode and taking action. You can pick any of these as per the situation and break the deadlock.

The 5 Second Rule, fear has a very deep-rooted relationship with postponing things. When you are afraid of doing something, its results, or have a distaste for it, the mind automatically starts over-thinking about it. It makes you think about the consequences if things go wrong and would also make you believe that something would go wrong. Many a time, if you don't act on time, the mind will be able to convince you that the time has passed and there is going to be no use of taking action then. The brain likes to keep you sitting tied to thoughts. That's the safest playing ground as per the account.

We only postpone things for the future that we don't like to do. People don't want to get up in the morning even though the alarm clock rings several times and gets snoozed. The reason is their dispassion for getting up. They don't feel excited about the prospects of the day. The same people would get up hours early if they have to do something about which they are passionate.

However, you can't be passionate about everything you need to do. Especially not about the things you fear or loath. Yet, inaction will only push you into overthinking.

Make it a rule to get into action within 5 seconds of having the thought. It is a concise window. But, you don't need to finish the job in 5 seconds. You simply need to initiate.

For instance, if you need to go to the office, within 5 minutes of the ringing of the alarm clock, you must be off the bed. Any longer you stay there, and your first preference would be to snooze it one last time. Once you cross the 5 seconds window, your mind would start overthinking the whole process and would surely find things to prove the futility of the entire process.

Get into action before it is too late. It is a great way to break the shackles of procrastination.

Most of the decisions taken by us are not conscious decisions. They are the decisions made on instinct. We don't put much thought into them. It happens because our mind remains on an autopilot mode most of the time.

If you have not been taxing it much about making real decisions, it likes to make decisions based on references. The things you did in similar situations earlier. Did they lead to any adverse outcome? What probability of success does it see for the actions in this attempt?

The mind doesn't like to see the probability of the success this time and the conditions that might lead it to the result. It wants to maintain inertia. It is the reason most people procrastinate and never take action. Their mind quickly disqualifies most of the possibilities without even considering them a little. The remaining time you'll have at hand now will get utilized for overthinking.

If you want to ditch this trap of overthinking, you

must ditch the autopilot. Look at the things mindfully. Take all the decisions consciously. Look at the merit of every situation, and don't try to assume things a lot. It will prepare a better ground for action, and it will also spare you from overthinking when you stop expecting a lot.

One of the biggest reasons for our backing down from taking any kind of action is our tendency to look at things pessimistically. We begin on a negative note and then expect things to end positively. It rarely works. The negative thought process is disheartening, and it is terrible for the initiative. Chiding your mind will not pump you up; it will push you into inaction.

Try to start anything new, even a day with positive intent. Don't weigh it down with expectations as that may also fill you with worries. Simply set out with a positive note that things would get better from where you start.

If you feel that positively looking at things from your perspective is not possible due to your limited view, try changing your perspective. Put yourself into the shoes of someone else you could imagine doing a better job at it. Think it through with a different perspective. Sometimes, changing the angle can bring all the change in the work.

Once a man was looking for a famous church in a village. He had come walking from far and was getting grumpy. He saw a boy paying in the way and asked him the distance of the church. I have come looking for it from so far. Sometimes we simply look at things from a tight angle. Looking at it through someone else's perspective can change the whole story. It can make the work easy and exciting. If you feel stuck at some action and feel that you do not have to go there, try thinking differently from the angle of someone else. Fears can push us into inaction. It has a powerful impact on our decision-making skills. If we don't address our concerns, it will keep cornering us. Even if we keep avoiding the fears, our mind doesn't sit silently; it makes you think all the time only about those fears and consequences of the actions.

There is no escape from this cycle. If you want to avoid it, the only practical way is to acknowledge your fears. The moment you recognize the concern, they lose the deadly impact they have. You can clearly understand the kind of impact they'll have. You also get a chance to look beyond the fears and assess the chances of success.

It is an excellent way to break the deadlock and come out of the habit of procrastination led by fear.

Our mind is continually looking for avenues to push us into inactivity. It seeks ways to push you into inaction, as that is the safest approach. Many people who began working ambitiously at one point end up in failures not because they had put in the poor effort but because their mind was able to convince them of the futility of their actions.

For instance, you aim to lose 30 pounds and get slim. Your aspirations, external motivations, and inspirations can energize you to begin work in that direction. But, it is a task that requires constant motivation as you will be working against your body. The body would make your job difficult. The mind would assist the body in it. It means that after a few days, maintaining that motivation can get very difficult. The task of 30 pounds is not something that you are going to get within a few days or weeks, and hence there is a high probability that you'll surrender.

Many people surrender even before they have begun as their mind starts overthinking about the probabilities of success and find none. Now, think if you had defined your goal more accurately and broken it down into smaller milestones. You'll lose 30 pounds in 6 months looks like a much well-defined goal. There is a target timeline so that you can't keep postponing it further. It is your first challenge to procrastinate.

However, six months is a very long period, and maintaining motivation, even with a defined goal, can be difficult. You also need milestones to help you in your pursuit. Signs help you in staging the results in smaller compartments so that you can track your progress. You need to lose 30 pounds in 6 months means that you have 24 weeks to lose 30 pounds. It brings us to 1.25 pounds per week. You will have a weekly target, and that can act as your constant motivator. You will have some weeks in which the weight loss would be slower. The milestones would push you to work harder the following week for making up for the deficit.

There will be weeks when your achievements will be higher, and the milestones will pump up to work harder for achieving the final goal faster. Quiet setting clear goals, dividing them into smaller milestones, and getting into action can help you in breaking the chains of procrastination and inactivity. Keeping a journal is a great strategy to help organize your thoughts. People tend to underestimate the power of noting down their dreams every day. Journaling enables you to rid your mind from things that you might not be aware of. It enhances your working memory and also guarantees that you can effectively manage stress. Therefore, you create space to experience new things in life. The effect of this is that you can relieve yourself from the anxiety that you might have been experiencing. The ideas or feelings or passions we wake up each day to pursue—our purpose.

7

FOCUS ON SOLUTIONS AND WHAT YOU CAN CONTROL

*W*e all worry from time to time. It is instinctual, as animals must worry about their hunger until they feed themselves. However, there is a certain point where worrying is unhealthy. If you find yourself continually worrying to the extent where it takes over your life, you need to take action. You must be able to enjoy your life. While you will undoubtedly worry occasionally, it should not prevent you from completing your daily tasks. When worrying becomes severe, it needs attention.

You must learn to stop worrying. There is always the chance of an adverse event occurring, but you must be able to find positivity and hope instead of dwelling on the potential for something going wrong.

You must be able to live in the moment and focus on enjoying yourself instead of worrying about what you did incorrectly in the past and what could go wrong in the future. You must be able to enjoy your life, not spend every minute of it worrying. It's essential to be able to stop the "what-ifs" and develop the ability to focus on the best possible outcome. There is a right balance between being realistic and being positive, and you must be able to find that balance. You should also become more aware of yourself and your emotions.

It sounds simple enough: just stop worrying. Although this seems easier said than done, it is possible to train your brain to worry less and be able to enjoy yourself more. However, this will take a lot of practice and patience with your progress. If you tend to worry naturally, this will be an ingrained habit that will take time to replace with better habits. You must be able to change your mind so that you may reduce the amount of worrying that you do.

There are a few ways that you can reduce the amount of time that you spend worrying. One way is to set aside time to worry simply, instead of suppressing your worries and ignoring them until they reach the point where they overwhelm you, set aside time each day to let your emotions happen simply. Instead of fighting against them, allow yourself to feel everything. You may even imagine yourself overreacting; this will enable you to see how beneficial (or not) it can be to allow your emotions to take over. Spending some time each day just letting it out will help you. You may choose to keep a journal or simply write everything down. Perhaps you type it out all of your thoughts and erase it right afterward so that you can see a clearing of your dreams right in front of you. You may choose to confide in someone you trust, allowing yourself to rant for a few minutes to get it all out. Regardless, it is healthy to let your emotions out instead of suppressing them.

Determine the root of your worries. Perhaps you have too much free time and simply need something else to occupy your mind. You may choose to take up a hobby to keep yourself busy. There may be a particular event that triggers your worries. You may feel worried while scrolling through social media, as you compare yourself to others and worry that you aren't good enough. Perhaps your fears are the result of a past trauma that you still haven't moved on. No matter the cause, it is essential to take some time to reflect on why it is that you worry and work on a solution for that.

Another aspect to consider is whether your

worries are solvable or not. If the concern has a solution, come up with a way to solve it and get it done. Instead of dwelling on it, explain it so that you may have more peace of mind. For unsolvable worries, you must be willing to accept that fact. Instead of trying to predict adverse said events or worrying about possibilities with a low likelihood, take the uncertainty. Will worrying solve it or change it? The answer is, most likely, "no." Worrying won't prevent unpleasant surprises. You must be willing to accept the fact that life continually changes. Finding the good in these changes can help you to be happier and stress less. Learning to live in the moment can help you to stop worrying. Often, suffering is a result of the past or future. We don't typically worry as much about what we are doing in the present. You must be willing to accept the past and live without regrets. Every mistake is a learning opportunity, and every issue will only make you stronger. The future is unpredictable; the best you can do is to work your hardest towards making it a future you want. However, that's pretty difficult when you spend your time worrying!

You must learn to enjoy the present, or else you will never enjoy your life. Tomorrow never comes, though. It will always be today. As a result, you must learn the importance of living today. Focus on the present. Be aware of all of the positive aspects of the present. To do this, you may have to shut off your electronic devices and take in your surroundings. Take a moment to realize how great today is and be more mindful. Accept your thoughts of the present, while allowing yourself to shut off thoughts about the past or future. Become aware of your senses. What are you seeing, hearing, smelling, feeling, and tasting? Instead of continually multitasking, take a moment to appreciate what you are doing.

The smallest details can make the most significant difference in your happiness. Appreciate everything, even the most minor aspects of life. You may live in the moment by being happier and bringing joy to others. Remember to laugh and smile. These can boost your happiness and help you to enjoy life more. Bring happiness to others, as well. Volunteering and performing small acts of kindness can go a long way. You will feel happy knowing that you made a difference and have a purpose. Be thankful for everything that you have, and be sure to help others that may need help as well. Occasionally take a moment to realize everything that you are thankful for. Find positivity every day. Take small moments to yourself. Perhaps you may choose to meditate. You may also simply breathe and focus on your breath. Focus on how your body feels and take some time to relax. You may think that you can't enjoy the present because you are too overwhelmed. Check with yourself regularly and remind yourself to live in the present. You will have to make a conscious effort to do this at first, as it is natural to visualize the future or dwell on the past. When you can live in the present, you will learn to enjoy life no matter how it is.

Self-awareness can help you. It can make it much easier for you to understand your emotions and feel more in control of your mind. You will realize why you act and think the way that you do. You can guess what your strengths and weaknesses are. It will also help you understand what motivates you. You will become more aware of your purpose and goals in life. It can even help you to understand others better and improve your communication skills. By increasing your self-awareness, you will have a healthier mind and feel much better about yourself and your emotions.

To become more self-aware, you will have to make a conscious effort to do so at first. Take some time each day to reflect on how you are feeling. Understand your current emotions, the causes of them, and the effect they have on you. You may also reflect on your day as a whole. Did you accomplish what you set out to do? If not, what held you back from doing so? Use this time to criticize yourself constructively. Do not merely criticize yourself, compare yourself to others, or think about how you failed. Instead, realize what worked for you and what did not. Doing so will benefit you, as you can learn from that and apply it to the next day. You will not be perfect at first, but if you can make improvements each day, you will be much better off. Only compare yourself to who you were yesterday. You should always be learning, improving, and changing for the better. It is a natural way to progress in life, and it's essential to do so to be the best person that you possibly can be. Remember to think about both what can be improved and what you did well, as it is essential to remind yourself of your successes and remember that you are capable of achieving.

You may ask others to help you in several ways. One way is to talk out your emotions with another that you trust. It can help you to express your thoughts verbally. You may also ask others for feedback, as they will be able to give you an opinion outside of yourself. However, this must be healthy. You should trust the other person's word and ensure that you take everything they say as a way to improve, not as an attack on the person that you are.

It's also vital that you can write down your values and goals. It will make you more aware of what you're working towards. If you don't have goals to work towards, you will lack both direction and a sense of purpose in life. Understand what is important to you and what gives you a sense of importance. If you don't have goals, you won't be able to reflect on your progress towards achieving your goals. As a result, you won't be able to be aware of how you are doing.

It's essential to stop your habit of worrying, and there are a few ways that you can work on it. You must, however, keep in mind that it will take work to stop yourself from worrying. It's also essential to discover how to live in the moment so that you can enjoy life and feel greater happiness. Stopping the "what-ifs" that you think can help you. Most of these are unnecessary, and you will feel better for not considering these thoughts. Finally, you must become more aware of yourself to worry less. It's great to learn tips and tricks that we can use to wrestle anxiety and excessive worry.

What will be the effect of thinking the way that you are thinking right now? Do these thoughts make you feel empowered to solve the problem at hand, or do they discourage you from believing in yourself and feeling capable of facing the issue at the side? Are there instances where your worries are valid? Yes! Sometimes we worry about things that are likely to happen. In this situation, what you will need to do is to face your worry and do something about it if you can.

If not, you may need to let it go. For those who are experts when it comes to worrying, this may seem impossible. However, you could say to yourself, "There is absolutely nothing that could be done to alter this right now." Then you can find some other activity for occupying your mind and distracting you from this situation that you have no control over.

Is There a True Problem to Solve? -then you might have to focus your attention on a practical solution for it. In this case, you might turn to problem-solving skills to deal head-on with the things that are worrying you.

Note: Anxiety is not your fault. Daily life and comes with stressors that can affect a person's thoughts, feelings, and everyday functioning!

Just like all other basic emotions, anger is designed to convey a specific message to us. That message could be our disapproval of something that has happened or something that someone has done. However, if our first response when angry is to vent or become raging mad, then the message gets lost in translation. For this reason, a calm mind and level-head are essential when dealing with anger. Being in a calm state of mind allows you to take a step back and objectively evaluate your passion from the point of reason. It also allows you to acknowledge your feelings and validate them without letting them control you.

Keeping calm when angry, however, is easier said than done. It takes a lot of practice, patience, and maturity to keep yourself from acting out of character when something that triggers rage in us happens. If someone offends you, it is much easier to get revenge. In a way, we derive some pleasure from causing suffering to perceived opponents when we feel like they have wronged us. In reality, however, these solutions are illusory, since they do not deal with the real issues and cause of our anger. They can be more detrimental to us and our relationships in the long run. In light of this, we must find healthier ways to control our anger, even when we feel justified in it.

So, what is anger management, and what does it entail? Mostly, anger management is the process of identifying signs that you are becoming angry or frustrated and taking the necessary steps to calm yourself down to deal with your anger more productively. Many people have the misconception that anger management is meant to keep you from feeling angry. Others even think that it is designed to help them suppress feelings. Both of these are poor understandings of the role of anger management. The purpose continually of anger management is to help you become better at identifying signs that you are becoming frustrated and equip you with the necessary skills to keep your anger under control. A lot of literature has been written about violence and how to deal with it more effectively. One can, therefore, learn the right skills for coping with frustration from reading books such as this one. However, the most common way through which people learn anger management is by attending an anger management class or therapy with a counselor.

You will get to learn how to identify the warning signs when you get frustrated, and how you can effectively calm yourself down to approach your anger from the point of strength.

While anger is a very normal reaction which may provoke feelings of aggression, using violence to deal with anger is very inappropriate. It can also lead to severe legal consequences, such as getting sued or imprisoned for abuse. If you find yourself prone to committing acts of violence when angry, you should seek professional help immediately. Through counseling and attending anger management classes, you can break this cycle of poor anger management and learn to express your frustration in healthier ways that do not involve the use of violence.

Perhaps you are not outrightly violent towards other people when angry. However, you may tend to smash or break things when angry. It is still not an appropriate response or strategy to deal with anger and frustration. This type of behavior fails to address the real cause of the rage, and only reinforces the idea that showing aggression is going to make the anger go away. The truth is that it doesn't work. The only effective way of dealing with anger is by getting to the root cause and harnessing the emotion in positive ways.

Another tell-tale sign that you need lessons in anger management is you find yourself constantly avoiding scenarios that may trigger your anger. Perhaps you don't like going to parties with your spouse because they always leave you alone to chat with other people. Or maybe, you avoid talking to one of your close friends because you feel they are too judgmental.

Whichever the case, the temptation to avoid any scenario that may trigger your anger can be too strong to resist. However, opting out of certain situations due to fear of getting frustrated is not an effective way of dealing with your anger. For one, it shifts the responsibility to the other person, thereby diminishing your power to take responsibility for your emotions. It also only covers up pent up frustration, which continues to simmer without your awareness. It can eventually erupt in very damaging ways, both to you and your relationships.

Anger management classes are to help people develop the skills to notice when they are getting angry and take the necessary steps to deal with the emotion appropriately. Usually, the classes are conducted as one-on-one sessions or group sessions with a counselor or therapist. Depending on your needs, the anger management program may take a few days, weeks, or even months in some cases. It is, therefore, essential for you to be patient and consider the whole experience as a learning process.

When you first begin attending anger management classes, the first thing you will learn is how to identify stressors and triggers of anger. By identifying the early warning signs of irritation, you can begin to understand its causes and figure out how to control it. Stressors are typically those things that cause frustration in your life and trigger pent up anger. These may include failure with a child who behaves poorly, financial problems, or co-workers who always gossip about you.

Apart from identifying the triggers, anger management classes will help teach you how to pick up on symptoms of anger. As we found out earlier, physiological signs of irritation vary between individuals. You may, therefore, not manifest the same symptoms as someone else when angry. While one person may experience an increased heart rate and sweat when angry, another person may feel a tight-knot in their stomach when upset. Anger management classes will help you identify the physical symptoms of anger as they present uniquely in your body.

Beginner's anger management is to help you recognize the signs that your anger is on the rise. Perhaps you may feel like you want to yell at the perceived object of your hatred, or you feel the need to keep quiet to avoid a heated confrontation. Being aware of the physical reactions happening in your body will allow you to take a step back and carefully evaluate your anger before proceeding with an appropriate response.

The ghost of the past is tough to go. The harder we try to push it, the more resounding it gets. It comes to haunt at the most inconvenient times. It should come as no surprise that you always remember everything terrible that has happened in your life. Your mind is a terrific storage device. It has unlimited storage ability. Scientists believe that you can record more than 2.5 petabytes of data in your brain and still have space left for more. It translates to 300 million hours of video recording space. It means that all the things that have happened in your life, positive or negative, are recorded in your mind. However, your brain also has a strong response to negative thoughts as it feels the need to keep playing them, again and again, to keep you safe from falling into the same kind of situation. It is a survival mechanism designed for good.

The problem begins when your mind starts playing the negative things obsessively and makes it impossible for you to start fresh. It makes wiping the slate clean tight. Your mind clutter has a vital role to play in this. You let your past remain heavy on you. The solace of victimhood, the desperation to stay safe, and vulnerability are some of the strong reasons.

These feelings encroach your productive space. They leave no room for positive thinking.

It all happens because you are not mindful. You have allowed your mind to remain cluttered by negative experiences and want to be in a safe sanctuary.

Let's consider a small story. Once there was a farmer. He had a big farm but had terrible luck in the past harvests. Sometimes the yields got affected by droughts, and sometimes pest attacks killed the crop. The farmer decided he had had enough of this nonsense. He wouldn't bear this nonsense again as his crops were getting ruined anyway. So, he decided to play it safe and planted nothing. Was that a solution? It was not a solution. Earlier the farmer had a fear that his harvest would get affected by rain or pests. There was a possibility that he may not get the full yield. But, his actions made it a certainty that he will not get anything at all. Playing safe is sometimes the worst move. The baggage of the past does this to you.

If you let your mind and thoughts rule your world, then you will rot in a corner without ever seeing the light of the day. It will keep telling you that the world is full of dangers and risks.

8

EMBRACE YOUR FEARS

*L*earning from the mistakes of the past and letting it go is the only way to excel in this world. If your mind is cluttered with worries, it will never be able to learn and succeed. It will lack the required potential. A cluttered mind is never able to make the distinction between a safe decision and a fearful decision.

Safe decisions are based on reality. They have their basis on the possible consequences of choices, and they invoke remedial precautions. The farmer could have made alternative irrigation arrangements. He could have employed pest control measures. Even if he hadn't done any of these, the probability of getting a harvest was 50-50. But, he took a fearful decision of doing nothing. The result was a guarantee of having nothing at all. Poor choices come from your insecurities, and they keep getting stronger. If you do not learn to fight them, they will degrade you and make you subhuman with no capability to enjoy this life.

The power to think is what makes humankind superior to other species dwelling on this earth along with us. If you look closely, they do all the things similar to us. They are born, eat, grow, reproduce, and die, just like us. There is effectively no difference between us and other species. The only thing that makes us different is our ability to think.

If you feel that most of your thoughts are negative, depressing, and self-destructive, you are not alone. It is the malice that troubles most of the human race. But, negative thinking has deep roots in the survival mechanism of humanity, and it has taken millions of years of careful evolution.

We were ill-equipped to arrange food and were practically defenseless against the beasts. Carelessness could have got us killed any minute. Our mind developed a negative thinking process in which it could play all the negative scenarios to devise a safe outcome. It is more of a protection mechanism.

If one person in the clan got killed by a beast, the scenario wouldn't merely end there. Our mind would keep playing the script so that you can formulate a strategy to avoid such an outcome again. The memory played the same scenario; it invoked fear so that we didn't make the same mistake. It helped in our survival. This mechanism of having negative thoughts has protected us for thousands of years against all the odds.

If today you are having a similar negative thought process going on in your mind, then it isn't baseless. It has its roots in the very same survival instinct that enabled you to survive even in the fiercest situations. However, there is a line beyond which anything becomes toxic. If you let your brain run loose without any control, then it will keep playing fearful scenarios to prevent you from taking action. Your mind knows that the safest bet to survive is to remain in the shell. The outside world is unpredictable, and the forces are beyond control. However, becoming the slave of this mentality is dangerous.

You are simply scared to take any action, and your mind starts showing you the worst possible consequences. Excessive negative thought patterns forming in your brain are a part of mind clutter. Your mind is filled with too much negativity, and it reflects the same in negative thinking. It can be a dangerous thing if it goes unchecked. It can make you indecisive, frightened, and weak. You will never be able to bring that winning edge in yourself. Your risk-taking abilities will end, and you will become a fearful decision taker, which means you will take no decisions at all. It is a pathetic state to be in the first place. You will lose all the control over your life. Your imagination and past scenarios will start deciding the way of your life. It will take a toll on your personal and professional life, health, family, relationships and career, and more.

Every person has negative thoughts. Only a toddler or a madman can be free from fear and negative thoughts. They are open from fear, and it has no real meaning in their experience. You, as a sane person, have the experience, and hence, your mind will play negative thoughts about things, relationships, and events. The important thing is to remain conscious of negative thoughts. If you keep ignoring the negative thoughts, they'll become more vigorous. Even a small mistake will get played repeatedly and frighten you.

If you have negative thought patterns and the fright is overpowering you and clouding your judgment, then start consciously analyzing your negative thoughts daily. Every day devote a fixed amount of time to ponder over the problematic situations at hand and the best possible way out. It will ease your negative thinking pattern, and you will be able to work constructively.

Can't Undo Spilled Milk; Make Cheese Out of It. If there is a problem, then brooding over it will not help. Think of the ways to overcome it. On a day to day basis, we come across several situations that have gone beyond our control. Crying over them will not help our cause. The only way to deal with such cases is to devise ways to nullify their effect. If you are late to work, then either choosing fast transport could help or think of a better excuse. Brooding over getting late is not going to be of any help.

The same goes for negative thinking in real life. If you are having negative thoughts, then in place of going deep into the repercussions, think about the ways you can deal with the situation. If a negative thought pattern has started and it is bringing in front of all the wrong things, start thinking of the good things you want and list the ones you can make happen. You can only kill negativity with positivity, and you will have to make do with the situations at hand. Try to make the best of it.

Negative thoughts are a torment. They lead to stress and anxiety. It is well known that stress and anxiety have a detrimental impact on your physiological as well as psychological health. They act as triggers that begin several negative processes. Your body starts releasing stress hormones that lead to fat accumulation, lethargy, and heartburn, stiffness in muscles, and the works. Your body reacts poorly to these triggers.

Trying to ignore these thoughts is going to make you even more anxious as your mind knows that you are avoiding them. You should adopt a 3-step approach to deal with such negative thoughts.

Vent: Give a vent to these thoughts. Do not be scared to think about them. Let them come out in the clear. It will help you in clearly understanding the extent of negative thoughts. Nevertheless, they do not remain immersed in them. Simply ponder over them and get over with them.

Cap: Once you have acknowledged the full scale of the negative thoughts, it will be easier for you to understand their extent. They will be less scary. It is time you can put an end to them. Devise plans to counter these negative thoughts.

Strategize: You have the scale of the problem; you have an understanding of it, now you simply need a strategy to overcome it. It is the stage where you can get help from several directions. Think of the ways to deal with the problem.

If you keep punishing yourself with negative thoughts, they will continue intensifying. Do not do that to yourself. Deal with the problem in an organized manner. Clear the clutter of your mind, and you will be able to think better.

Writing down your negative thoughts is an excellent way to clear the clutter of your mind. If you keep playing the negative thoughts in your mind, they'll keep getting stronger. The same scenarios will keep getting repeated over and over again.

Write down the negative thoughts and get them off your mind. It will help you in sorting your mind. When one thing is less to mix, your mind is better capable of thinking. Nothing helps in decluttering the mind better than jotting down your thoughts on paper.

Negativity is a strong emotion. It gets expressed visibly and engulfs your thought process. The best way to deal with negativity is to embrace positivity. There may be a dozen negative things going around in your life at a particular moment, but it doesn't mean the absence of positivity. You will need to remind yourself of the positive things happening around you.

It will help in fighting your negative emotions. You should continuously remind yourself of the blessings in life. Think about the pleasant things in life to come. The things that you love or that infuse positivity. Take a break from the negative routine. Indulge yourself with some light moments. It will take off your brain from negative thoughts. You will be able to break the negative thought patterns easily.

Most of the time, negative thoughts are very imposing. They take off our minds from everything else. They instill fear. We are so frightened that we never pay attention to that extent. However, most of the time, we are so engrossed in the fear that we overestimate its potential. If negative thought patterns are arising and fear is gripping you, evaluate its merit. Look if it can cause the amount of damage that you think.

Measure the risks and answer your fears. Do not take negative thought patterns on their face value. Think of the positive outcomes of your actions and compare if they are higher than the risks. You will have better clarity of mind. Remaining lost in negative thoughts is not going to help your cause.

We live in the age of 24/7 news channel age. Most of the time, the news is not favorable as negativity sells fast and has excellent resonance. It is intriguing, and you feel like looking for more. It is the biggest reason why most of the news items are negative. From social media platforms to the internet in general, negativity is widespread. The idea is simple; negative news has a more significant impact than positive news. It creates curiosity that will lead to more TV time, more searches, more interest, and, ultimately, more revenue. But eventually, you are at the receiving end of this negativity. It gives a bad start to your day. One negative news can shift your mind to harmful gear. You can start reflecting on all the things going wrong in your life and relate them to the report.

You live in an age where information access is instant. Do not begin your day with the news. If you must, then look only for the story that concerns you.

It is essential to replace negative thoughts with positive ones; however, it is not as easy to do as it sounds. Most people misunderstand the whole idea of negative thinking. Happiness does not depend on a few negative thoughts; slightly, it might depend on how one handles these negative thoughts.

Despite any setbacks and obstacles, it is essential to try to maintain one's sense of optimism. The benefits of avoiding negative thinking are more significant than most people think. Actually, within the field of psychology, positive psychology is slowly gaining more attention. It involves the study of the physiological and psychological effects of positive thinking, behavior, and habits.

Research suggests that positive thinkers enjoy life more than pessimists do. When it comes to physiological and psychological health, in addition to stress levels, optimistic people are way ahead of the game. Thinking positively is an excellent way to heal; however, people need to understand that they should stop listening to the falsehoods their mind is telling them.

They should also try figuring out the origin of their negative thoughts. The first thing to remember is that negative thoughts stem from wrong assumptions and beliefs. Therefore, ignoring these thoughts is not good enough. Everyone is worthy of love and happiness, and people should always remember this fact.

It is natural for human beings to face stressful situations, such as job loss, domestic conflict, and more. How people deal with stressful situations makes all the difference. According to research, however, people who have a more optimistic outlook tend to approach difficult situations more positively.

Instead of wasting energy on negative thoughts

that one cannot change our thinking about things that went wrong, people who think in a positive way take the opposite direction. They understand they cannot change certain situations and find ways of dealing with life more positively.

Thinking more positively makes one less likely to experience problems such as depression and anxiety. According to experts, optimists enjoy a better quality of life, including psychological health, than pessimists do. Contrary to popular belief, positive thinking can cure certain mental behaviors and difficulties.

People who do not consider themselves do not need to worry. Overcoming negative thought patterns and starting to experience the benefits of positive thinking is not an impossible task. Stillness, for example, is a great way to overcome negativity. People can learn to break away from their negative thoughts through meditation. Some believe that only people who think positively can engage in healthy behavior, such as regularly working out. However, this is not always the case. Although they tend to have a higher motivation to exercise, even those with frequent negative thoughts can learn to focus on their physical health by eating better and getting regular workouts.

According to another theory, optimistic people tend to have better physical health because they are better able to handle stress, or maybe because they experience less stress. Thus, the adverse effects of stress on their physical health are significantly less. It is essential to stop worrying about one's negative thoughts to enjoy the following health benefits like live longer, Prevent cardiovascular diseases, Recover faster from illnesses and injuries, gain a more reliable immune system and better overall well-being.

It is common for people to believe that negative thoughts are harmful or even toxic, which is why so many people worry about their negative feelings. According to some "experts," negative thoughts lower people's positive vibrations, keep them stuck on negativity, and so on. Mostly, they teach people to banish their negative thoughts to gain confidence and feel self-assured.

Some online articles and self-help books seem to suggest that getting rid of negative thoughts equals professional success, higher vibration, inner peace, better boyfriend/girlfriend, and much more. Consequently, people who consistently experience negative thoughts tend to wonder what to do with the thoughts running in their minds.

They wonder how to make such thoughts stop, or

whether trying to force a positive impression over a negative one can work. Unfortunately, most people tend to misunderstand the whole issue of negative thinking because they do not understand what thoughts, both positive and negative, are in the first place. The negative feelings that people have do not determine their happiness; instead, it is what they do with those thoughts.

Countless thoughts pass through the human mind every day, and most of them are negative. It would be interesting to meet and talk with a human being who never has negative thoughts. Most people carry tons of harmful trash in their minds, even those that always seem positive.

For example, someone who is walking around congratulating himself/herself for buying a new car might be trying to disguise negative thoughts and reinforce the idea that he/she was not good enough before buying the new car. Essentially, having negative thoughts is a normal part of being human; therefore, people do not need to worry about having them in the first place.

People do not have to believe in their negative thoughts. Contrary to what one's mind would like one to think, not all ideas are correct. A person's mind is just a part of him/her; therefore, it is essential to separate one's thoughts from one's sense of self. The four components of a human being are Physical body, Mind, Spiritual aspect, and Heart.

One's mind, therefore, is simply a powerful tool for one to use, and one filters one's perceptions and thoughts through one's unique belief system. Negative thoughts stem from this filter because negativity is on the screen. Therefore, when people try to heal and grow, what they are doing is changing their filters or belief system. Everyone is perfect in his/her way; therefore, people do not need to analyze and worry about their critical and nasty thoughts. They are simply thoughts, and the only way to overcome them is to stop listening to them. When one's mind is in the moment of calm, one will feel content and at peace. It is possible when one refuses to believe one's negative thoughts.

There is nothing wrong with choosing positivity; however, it is essential to remember that negative thoughts do not matter in the first place because they are often untrue. Also, they do not make one a wrong person or a lesser human being. When people try to attack and reject their negative thoughts automatically, they are unconsciously telling themselves that they are not good enough. Mostly, according to them, reasonable people should not have negative thoughts.

This belief, however, is just as harmful as their initial thoughts.

The small step of identifying the negative thought and refusing to believe it is an essential step towards growth. Fortunately, the more one does this, the easier it will be to recognize negative thoughts when they appear, which will result in fewer negative thoughts.

Therefore, thinking positively is not the only way to find healing; rather, understanding that one is feeling bad because of entertaining and believing negative thoughts is the fastest way to heal and grow. It can also help determine the origins of one's negative feelings. However, since most of them stem from untrue beliefs, it might be easier to ignore them.

Worrying is a form of negative thinking. Thoughts tend to have powerful ramifications. When people have positive thoughts and stay positive, they tend to experience positive things. On the other hand, negative things tend to happen to people who entertain and believe their negative thoughts. By worrying excessively, people reinforce their negative attitudes and beliefs.

Unfortunately, the negative thoughts people focus on and worry about having a habit of coming true. People's thoughts and worries have a profound effect on their lives. By constantly worrying about a particular thing, people unwittingly spur it into becoming a reality.

Once people understand the correlation between worrying and negative thinking, they can begin to deal with their negative thoughts and change them. Consequently, they will start to focus on things, which will lead to positive outcomes in their lives.

Pro Tip: Self-awareness is one of the skills people should try to master or at least become more familiar and practiced before turning their energies to self-esteem and confidence. Without knowing where you stand psychologically, mentally, and emotionally, it is difficult to determine where your focus should be aimed and what kinds of goals you should set to reach your ultimate hopes and aspirations.

9

MANAGE YOUR STRESS- MOVE, UNPLUG, AND SPEND TIME IN NATURE

*H*aving a bustling personality can make you feel pushed, restless, and over-powered. Fortunately, we've assembled a rundown of approaches to declutter your brain. The best spot to start to declutter your life is from within. Numerous individuals neglect the advantages allows a sound mind can offer. The mind can move towards becoming hindered with psychological weight and indeed sway an individual's capacity to work. Necessary leadership can turn into a test, and adapting to issues may feel unthinkable when you do not have a clear mental state; in this manner, it is imperative to figure out how to free your mind of excessive clutter.

At the point when you are attempting to keep

mental tabs on everything that is going on, your contemplations are probably going to get confused. Keeping in touch with them down will assist you with prioritizing what's most significant, which will make you feel less focused. You can check significant dates and updates on a schedule or in a scratch pad, and scribble down your musings on anything that is stressing you in an individual journal. It does not make a difference whether you utilize an application or simply get a pen and paper.

Work a portion of the tips recorded above into your regular day to day existence to enable you to offload mental mess. Ensure you get a touch of 'personal time' each day with the goal that you can slow down appropriately. Much the same as tidying up your room keeps it from transforming into an all-out dump, reflecting, composing, ruminating, and conversing with others consistently will help anticipate the development of messiness in your brain.

We have all heard that reflection is a decent method to clear your brain and unwind. What you might not have heard is that there are a vast number of approaches to be careful. It implies you can search for a way that suits you. Some regular things to attempt are yoga, exercise, and profound relaxation.

Some not conventional approaches to rehearse care are washing up, snuggling up, or chilling by the seashore. Do whatever works for you.

It is difficult to fix something if you do not know what's up. Know about admonition signs that your psyche is getting to be stuffed. Some typical things to watch out for are issue resting, poor fixation, and not able to unwind.

When you've perceived that your psyche needs a spring clean, the following stage is to discover what's adding to the messiness. Invest significant time to think about how you are feeling. It will assist you in identifying what's worrying you, and why. After some time, you'll improve at detecting the notice indications of a jumbled personality and have the option to halt things from the beginning pleasant and early.

Conversing with a confidant or relative, regardless of whether on the web or eye to eye, can be an extraordinary method to clear your psyche, discharge a few feelings and get whatever's irritating you out into the open. It additionally gets a new take on an issue that understands you puzzled and is worrying you. If you are genuinely battling, recollect that you do not need to handle your effects without anyone else. There are loads of different experts accessible to chat with about whatever's stressing you.

Keep in mind your past and develop from it. You can expect that on occasion you will slip once again into old examples. Ordinarily, Those examples have been preparing for a considerable length of time. Stress and blame specifically are complicated feelings. At the point when you get yourself in an old pattern, ask yourself, "How's my self-talk?" If you wind up drenched in tension, separate your stresses into two classifications: those you can control and those you cannot.

Guide yourself to Stop! Whenever stress rings a bell, or you verbalize it for all to hear, guide yourself to stop! Supplant negative considerations with positive ones. One case of a definite idea is a token of what you do have rather than what you need. It isn't just about cash yet, Also, your aptitudes, gifts, capacities, companions, family, and supporters.

In essence, making a concerted effort to clear your mind of clutter is a tremendous first step that you can take toward getting a handle on overthinking. As you begin to sort out through the fluff, you will be able to make better sense of your life and, most importantly, about the people around you. Bear in mind that if people are feeding that clutter, then it might be time to move away from them.

Schedules lighten a portion of your mental stress by making a timetable. When you have all assignments sorted out and arranged out, with spare time included between, a significant measure of strain will be lifted. You will live more proficiently and suffer from less overpowering minutes. You cannot get ready for everything, and calendars must be changed now and again. In any case, having a reliable schedule for the things you realize you should do, organized by significance, can have a considerable effect on your mental stress. Besides, this is an incredible method for promising you to have time put aside to rehearse your mind-decluttering systems.

Meditation is a famous instrument to help declutter your life and your mind. You do not need to think as it was done in the good 'old days. Attempt this increasingly modernized system: start with music you appreciate. A few people profit by uplifting tunes or great songs, while others may prefer something edgier. The class is altogether up to you, and it does not need to be unwinding music. Next, locate a place where you can disengage yourself from others and diversions.

Written words are an integral asset to declutter your life. How you utilize them is up to you. A few people prefer to write in a diary. It can be private, and nobody else needs to see it. If you are worried about others discovering your written musings, consider writing them down on a piece of paper and after that discarding it or demolishing it after you are finished.

Start to declutter your life presently, beginning with your mind. You will feel better, work all the more adequately, and suffer from fewer misfortunes. Besides, when terrible things occur, you will be better prepared to deal with them when your mind is clear of clutter!

There is a lot of power in being positive. You can make a big difference in the lives of others by being positive. You wake up in the morning on Monday and think to yourself: "I can do it! I look forward to this new day of work. It is going to be great. I took my shower and had my coffee. Now I'm ready to go."

When you see that you can contribute something positive to this world, you will be able to adjust your attitude and expectations. Think about this: our lives are too short for us to worry about things that are frivolous and empty. We should not go through our days and complain about every little thing in our lives.

Granted, many things are worth complaining about, such as a meal that takes too long to prepare at a restaurant, the gossip that's going around in your office, among other things. We can easily break down and gripe about these things. For this reason, we want to guide you through every step of cultivating a positive attitude and changing your approach to various situations in your life.

The first thing that you have to recognize is that there are a lot of challenging situations in life. Nothing worth much is going to come quickly. Sometimes, you have to rough it through the tough times to feel better about your experience. It always takes a lot of hard work and dedication to reach your goals. And often, we do not reach our goals because we are downcast from all the expectations that we put on ourselves or others put on us. In the middle of all this, we worry about getting our dreams and goals. When you have the end goal in mind, you can move forward with your life and edge one step closer to the milestone that is going to change your life. Perhaps, your goal is to set aside $3,000 for your next vacation, or you want to become healthier and work out so you can overcome depression and live a better lifestyle. Or maybe you wish to pay off a student loan, so you work hard. Sometimes, we just have to be more straightforward about our goals because only then can we have more realistic expectations of the ones that will lead us forward.

You may now be wondering how it is that you can get into a positive mindset. Well, it is a lot easier than you might think. The first thing that you should do is get a pen and paper and write down fifteen things that you are thankful for. You will see what influences your thoughts when you get a feel of the things that make you feel grateful allows.

Practicing gratitude is one of the most powerful things you can do in your life. It helps you get out of tough times when you feel stuck and unable to move forward. Also, it helps you to get out of depression when you have a situation of losing a job or some catastrophe that throws you a curveball. As a result, you might feel helpless or devastated. But when you write down the thing that you are thankful for, you will realize just how blessed you are and how joyful you can be. Life is a precious gift. When you realize how many things have been handed to you, you see that you have the support of numerous people who want to get you out of your struggles and into a more prosperous life. Think of the people who love you, including your friends, parents, siblings, and other people. Also, think about the financial situation that you have been given and the job that you go to every day. Think about these blessings and remove any kind of feeling of entitlement that you might feel toward those blessings. You should recognize that you receive a lot more than you truly deserve and that everything is a gift of grace. Instead of griping about the lack of money that you have in your bank account, take a moment to say thank you to a person who has changed your life for the better and practice gratitude. Believe that it will change your day and make it a better one.

Stop right now and get your pen and paper. Write down the things you are thankful for.

Now that you have taken that step, you can come back and realize that you are on your way to becoming a positive person. Recall a time when you met success. Perhaps you got an A in your calculus class in high school, although you did not actually like math but rather enjoyed studying it. Or in university, perhaps you landed a top-notch internship at a Fortune 500 company that eventually led to a full-time position there. Maybe you were able to get healed from a psychological disorder that you had for a long time. You had a miracle healing experience. Be thankful and recall the times that have gone by and how you managed to overcome different situations. Think about how strong you have become in overcoming all the difficulties that have come your way. Not everyone can fight the good fight the way you have. Having different psychological and physical conditions can be hard, and when you feel that you are depressed, even getting out of bed can seem like a hard thing. Once you can get over something big, you can recognize that you did it well, and you can celebrate.

Now that you have a grateful mindset, you are ready to change the world, and one of the best ways to do that is by helping others. When you help others, you can improve your feelings and mood more than anything else. For example, when you help an elderly lady put her groceries in her car and move the cart away, you have done something to help someone else. It can increase your self-esteem and make you feel good.

Helping others is also a form of therapy that helps you to make a positive impact in others' lives while improving your overall emotional well-being. When you develop a positive mindset, you can make a big difference in other people's lives. For example, you could smile and look at yourself in the mirror and say to yourself, "See, you are doing well! You are going to have a good day!" Then you will immediately feel better. It allows you to be filled with positive vibes, which help you to keep going in your mind.

The positive hero mindset can become even more powerful when you laugh. When you tell a joke and make others laugh or watch Robin Williams or some other comedian on Netflix and laugh your bottom off, you can instantly infuse a place with positivity and fight off those feelings of negativity. All of this will give you more positive attitudes and allow you to feel at your best. You should feel like you can be playful, glad, and thankful all at the same time. Being a positive hero can make you a light in the middle of the darkness that pervades this life. As we have already stated, there is a lot to be sad and depressed about in this world; however, you can make up for it by making the world a better place by adding bits of positivity, making people laugh and smile and give others a high-five from time to time. It will change your whole mindset and provide you with joy that you never thought you had in you before.

I'm not trying to paint the picture with bright colors only. It is hard to be positive sometimes. You have to suffer a lot in this life from the cares and worries of mundane everyday routine. Some days, you may lie in bed and think, "Why should I bother about all this? I do not want to go to work today." But what if I told you that it is possible to get rid of your crippling self-doubt and start living in a more positive and bright mindset every day? You can do it! I know you can.

10

BE GRATEFUL AND HAPPY

There are a few additional tips and tricks for you to be aware of to help you to make better progress towards your goals and to make it easier for you to accomplish what you want to. You may work on improving your health, as it affects everything you do. Having the proper mindset will also help you, as you can accomplish more and feel better when you have the appropriate mindset. You may also learn some additional tips and tricks regarding goal-setting and how to establish new habits.

You may learn how to improve your mental and physical health. Your health affects everything that you do. When you are physically healthy, you will have more motivation and energy so that you can accomplish more. You will feel better and feel more motivated to get out and make progress towards achieving your goals. Your physical health directly affects your mental health. If you are physically healthy, you will feel more confident. Having good physical health will also help you to recognize that you are capable of achieving your goals. When you are mentally healthy, you will be less stressed and anxious. You won't worry as much, and you will be able to focus more on what's important. You will be in a better place and be able to make decisions better. You will also improve your relationships with others and communicate more effectively. The following are some tips and tricks for improving your health.

Find out if you are the proper weight. The best way to do so is to consult a medical professional. If you are overweight or obese, you are significantly increasing your risk for a variety of health problems, and you must take action and make progress towards being your ideal weight. Being overweight can increase your risk for health conditions, as well as physical injuries and pain. When you are not physically healthy, you will not feel as well and will feel unmotivated to get out and accomplish your goals. You may also feel self-conscious and lack confidence in yourself as a result.

Practice morning and night-time routines. By having a set routine in the morning, you are starting on the right foot and setting yourself up for success. It will get you in the right headspace to be productive throughout the day. You may take a shower, eat breakfast, go for a run, go over your to-do list, or whatever it is that helps you to get motivated and ready for the day. Having a night-time routine is excellent so that you can unwind, relax, and get ready for bed. It will help you to fall asleep faster and stay asleep throughout the night. It can help you if you are stressed, anxious, or tend to overthink. You may also establish a skincare routine so that you take care of your skin correctly. Do not forget to use sunscreen every day as well so that you can protect your skin daily.

There are some other simple ways to improve your health. Going to bed at a decent time can help you to get a proper amount of sleep. Having good posture can improve your muscular fitness. Doing puzzles and reading books are great ways to stimulate your mind. Swapping out junk food for more nourishing food will fuel your body more effectively. Making simple exercise swaps such as taking the stairs instead of the elevator and parking farther will get you to exercise a bit more. Also, remember to stretch regularly (and after using) to avoid injury and increase your flexibility.

Your mindset can make or break you. If you have the proper mindset, you will view life much more positively. You will be able to bounce back quickly after hitting an obstacle or having an issue. You will see the world as a much more positive place with infinite room to grow and improve. It will also be easier for you to find motivation and push yourself to work towards your goals. You will enjoy learning and bettering yourself, and it will be easy for you to establish new habits and live a healthier life. The proper mindset can make a world of difference for you.

To improve your mindset, you can start your day with positive affirmations. Tell yourself how wonderful you are. Remind yourself of your achievements and the strengths that you have. You may also focus on what you are grateful for and everything good in your life. Remember to laugh. To cope with adverse situations, find humor, and enjoy a good laugh. The entity does not have to be so severe, after all. Remember that failures make the most significant lessons, and you can learn from your mistakes. Think highly of yourself and learn to live with no regrets. Even if you could have done something, you didn't. Everything happens for a reason, and everything that has happened in the past has led to this moment. Appreciate that and learn to focus on the present instead of the past (or worrying about the future). Surround yourself with people that have the mindset that you want.

To work on improving your mindset, you may practice breathing, which will allow you to focus more and simply relax. You may also reflect on your thoughts to check your emotions. Write down anything you are thinking: your worries, anything you need to do, what you love about life, your goals. Sometimes, it's good to have your thoughts written down. Always remember to set goals for the next day so that you have something to work towards and achieve. Switch up what you listen to. Maybe your drive to work is usually silent. In that case, you may want to try a podcast to inspire you. Listen to what makes you feel happy and motivated.

Focus on your language. Is there a way to change the way you speak to be more positive? Become mindful of this. Start reading! You can educate yourself and learn about a new topic or get sucked into a good story and lose yourself in the book. Learn what emotional outlet works for you. Instead of suppressing your emotions, practice healthily dealing with them. Reward yourself for your successes.

When you accomplish a goal, make good progress, or have another success, take time to recognize your achievement and reward yourself for your excellent work. It will keep you motivated and ready to accomplish more. You will start associating your goals with happiness and rewards. Remember to smile. Surround yourself with people that make you laugh and smile and remember to do what makes you happy.

Setting goals can be hard! You may not know where to start, what you want to accomplish, or how to set your goals appropriately. Establishing habits may also be tricky, as you must incorporate something new into your life and stick with it.

Core values are convictions and beliefs that people adopt as their guiding principles in their daily activities. They are behaviors that people choose to exercise as they pursue what is right and what humankind expects of them.

Core Values have the following characteristics: they can be specific, they can be different from culture to culture, they can bring disharmony between different people, a person can learn values early in life from family or friends, and finally values are often emotive.

Core values are of different types. Some of the

classes include family, moral, social, socio-cultural, material, spiritual, environmental, intellectual, financial, and self-care values.

Examples of core values that emanate from the classification above include respect, honesty, freedom, fearlessness, dignity, loyalty, trust, cooperation, concern for others, initiative, justice, peace, humor, generosity, adventure, friendships, and excellence.

Core values are vital because they reflect people's needs, desires, and the things they care about most in life. Core values are remarkable uniting forces for people's identities. Core values are also decision-making guidelines that help people to connect to their authentic self.

Core values are vital factors that lead to the growth and development of individuals. The benefits help people to live happier lives, doing what is most important to them.

The following are the reasons why people need to develop personal core values.

Core values help people to acquire information about their strengths and weaknesses. That is because self-awareness comes from a person being honest with himself or herself about who he or she is.

Honesty is a value that facilitates people to talk about themselves truthfully. In that way, people can appreciate both their strengths and weaknesses. Honest people do not try to make themselves appear better than they might be. The value of wisdom enables people to understand themselves better and to accept what they cannot change. It also helps people to realize that they cannot expect success if they do not know how to use their abilities. Humility is a core value that brings a person to appreciate what other people are doing. A humble person allows other people to be in the limelight and to celebrate their successes. An ordinary person will not focus on himself or herself at the expense of other people.

Core values help people to learn about themselves so that people can live meaningful lives.

Core values point to the way a person should go. Core values are about standards that define who people think they are and what they hold in high esteem. While people cannot always measure up to these standards, the ideals tell them how they should think and act.

In the professional world, employers run businesses in unethical manners. Such unethical practices include lying about the effectiveness of a product or having mission statements that do not align with the company's conduct.

A person who follows his or her values will not do things just because other people think it is OK to do so. Core values help people to check whether they are consistent with what they believe is essential.

Core values inform people's thoughts, feelings, words, and, ultimately, actions. A person's values help to explain his or her actions. A person who values honesty strives to be honest. Accordingly, a person who values transparency will always try to be transparent. When it comes to material things, a person who values his or her family dedicates his or her time to be with family members, and he or she encourages family relationships. Similarly, a person who values fitness will more likely develop daily rituals and long-term habits that promote fitness.

In the corporate world, a person may act in ways that are consistent with his or her values. Since people have different values, conflict may arise in the workplace. However, companies try to instill common core values that will guide every person's behavior. For example, when hiring, a company may not control what shapes different people's values and ethics. However, the company may try to influence its employees through training programs and codes of conduct to get the employees to behave in ways that are acceptable to the company. Core values are thereby very crucial in determining and guiding behavior.

Core values make people see how unique and special each person is. Some people value adventure, while others value safety. Also, some people may value solitude, while others may value publicity. For example, a person who values solitude may feel smothered if he or she allows his or her friend to influence them to go out for a party. The person may agree to go along, but they will not be having a great time. For the friend, people, drinks, and endless conversations may be their lifeline.

Everyone is different, and what makes one-person ecstatic may leave the other person feeling disconnected and uneasy. Consequently, a person has to know their values and live by them without fear of the unknown.

A meaningful conversation is one where the parties involved are present in the moment and not distracted by thoughts or by other people's activities. Also, a meaningful discussion includes people being open, transparent, and willing to share their honest thoughts and feelings.

When a person is not open to say what he or she thinks or feels, they are most likely not having a candid conversation. Values of transparency, honesty, openness, and genuineness help people to communicate meaningfully.

Meaningful conversations also value sensitivity. Sensitivity means that a person can sense people's needs to talk about painful experiences, and he or she is asking them about it. When a person opens up about an awkward situation, the listening party should sit quietly, listen keenly, and offer a piece of wisdom when necessary. Care for other people is a value that can go a long way in making people feel better about themselves. All it takes is one meaningful conversation about changing another person's life.

A person's core values affect every part of his or her life. Most of the time, a person's interests come from their life experiences and the people closest to him or her.

If a person values spending time with his or her spouse, but he or she has to work for extended hours, the person will experience internal conflict and stress. In such an event, the person needs to go back to his or her values to seek help.

The values will help the person to understand his or her topmost priorities in life, and in that way, he or she will determine the best decision to make for himself or herself. For a person to become the best person that he or she can be, the person has to live in agreement with his or her values. As a result, the benefits will be the foundation for the person's goals and life purpose.

Confidence becomes easy to achieve when a person is clear on his or her core values. When a person is not bright on what he or she benefits, they feel less confident to interact with other people.

Core values boost confidence in that they help a person to form ideas around what the person values. That is because people's core values shape their thoughts and opinions about issues. Every person's 'point of view' usually emanates from his or her value system. That is what brings about bias in conversations and other aspects of life.

Consequently, a person's core values help him or her have an opinion, or to stand out in a matter, or to have interesting conversations and interactions. A person who is not sure about his or her values, cannot have the courage and confidence to interact freely or to speak their mind.

Observe yourself and learn, you can begin by asking yourself the following questions: What two things were missing in my childhood?

Are there people in your life who you look up to?

You could be looking up to a family member, a friend, a grade school teacher, a university lecturer, a celebrity, a famous personality, or even the person who works at your favorite restaurant. Then ask yourself, 'why do I admire these people?' It could be that you marvel at the values they embody. For example, the person who works at your favorite restaurant is always smiling when serving others, and you can see that the person genuinely loves his or her job. Your grade school teacher ever listened to every student with sincerity, and you admired her excellent listening skills and charisma.

Identify the specific values that the people in your list exemplified. Those values can inspire you to adopt them.

Think back to the most painful moments of your life. Where were you? What made you sad? If you have experienced the pain of being excluded by others, then you may find that you value inclusivity and compassion. Although pain is an undesirable experience, it helps people to learn the things that they would not want to re-live. As a result, they develop values about what they consider significant. From pain, you may have developed values of tolerance and resilience, humility, empathy, and independence.

Think back to the most joyous moments of your Life- What were you doing? Why did that make you happy? Did other people share your happiness? Who were they? What other things contributed to your feelings of joy? As you recall those moments, find examples from your school, career, family, and personal life. You will discover that every experience is essential and valuable for the values that come with each lesson.

Make a list of your core personal values. First, write down a list of your core values. Afterward, go through the list, visualizing circumstances where each value may apply.

For example, when comparing the values of adventure and security, imagine that you have to decide to go to a different country to explore new opportunities, or continue to live where you are because it is a more familiar place. Continue working through your list until you identify values that resonate with you.

There is a secure connection between confidence, emotional control, and the conquering of psychological habits. Over the years, through all of the surveys, interviews, and studies conducted, this is the most common and repeated truth from those participating in them and those performing them: no matter what a person is trying to attempt, confidence is key!

There are lots of different life factors that can affect a person's self-esteem and confidence, with adolescence taking the most significant toll on a person's view of themselves. During puberty, humans It is in these years that men and women receive the majority of their emotional education as it has the highest inclusion of factors like the following for most people: First romantic relationships (often tumultuous with lots of highs and lows), First deep friendships that are tested by adjusting hormones, changing personalities and other life factors that may arise without warning, First significant successes and accomplishments like national awards and recognition, college scholarships and summer internships, Learning to drive and understanding the responsibility that comes with getting behind the wheel of a car and developing decision-making skills that are shaped by how adolescents handle things like peer pressure, balancing their school, work, and social lives, and making their first life-affecting decisions like if they want to further their education after their required schooling is completed.

With all of these exciting changes taking place,

how could someone's self-esteem and confidence levels be hindered or even damaged? Unfortunately, for all of the specific events men and women experience during their teenage years, there are also a lot of adverse events and factors they face (in their highest quantity and intensity than most people see throughout the rest of their lives) such as: Learning to differentiate affectionate teasing from friends and loved ones with harmful teasing and bullying that comes from those to cause harm, Physical changes to their skin, muscles and other parts of the body that may require attention from over-the-counter medical products or even prescriptions from medical professionals and Emotional modification said that is often unexpected, and out of control as skills are developed through experience and education, Lots of fear and uncertainty as everything seems to be changing around them without a sense of direction or stopping point insight.

Not everyone has come out of adolescence with more negative memories than positive ones, but for those that did and find those negative experiences or memories affecting their adult lives, never fear! The following are some tips and tricks for helping you with improving these.

To properly set goals, it's important to choose

goals that you feel passionately about. If you do not care about a goal, you are not likely to stick with it. The common proper goal is SMART. It should be specific, measurable, attainable, relevant, and time-bound. Be specific about what you want. Set a goal so that you can measure your progress. Make sure it is realistic for you to attain. Make it relevant to your interests and passions. Give yourself time to achieve that goal.

There are a few categories for goals that you may set for yourself. You may set educational purposes so that you may learn more. Psychological goals are essential for remaining emotionally stable and improving your mindset. These are all types of goals that you can set for yourself.

For getting started with new habits, you will have to make a change and make that change a part of your life. It will require you to get used to it and make it a natural part of your daily routine. To properly form habits, you should focus on only one to three patterns at once. Any more will overwhelm you, and you won't be able to dedicate yourself to them fully. Commit for at least thirty days. It is how long it will take for you to get used to your new habit or habits. Remind yourself. Perhaps a one activity that you already do should go along with your new practice. You may have to give yourself reminders for your new habit. Do not expect too much at once. You may ease into the original pattern and gradually make progress towards it. Plan for failure, and know what you will do when you face obstacles and how you won't let them get in your way. Tell others about your habit so they may hold you accountable for it. Reward yourself for making progress towards your practice. Finally, remember that you can change yourself. Accept and welcome change into your life. You cannot get better if you do not make a change.

CONCLUSION

Congratulations on reaching the final section of the book. Overthinking is not a mental disorder but leads to mental disease and psychological problems. Sometimes overthinking is a result of anxiety and depression, and sometimes stress and depression. When you start overthinking, you feel disturbed, and lots of thoughts gather in your mind ruminating repeatedly. You start making mistakes that you will not notice while doing but can physically and emotionally harm you. To prevent yourself from overthinking and overcoming your anxiety, stress, and depression, you need to follow simple habits that are described. Try to fit these habits in your daily routine, and these will help you relax your mind and make your day fresh and energetic. Thus, stop overthinking and do not evaluate yourself with other people's points of view. Just stand up for yourself and fight with your thoughts until you come out of these.

When you feel like your mind is full of thoughts, try to declutter your account using the simple habits discussed. Decluttering your mind will help you to enhance your mental wellbeing. The point is, you might get back to overthinking ruminating over and over again. It will help if you learn to relax and settle your mind to keep it from continuously circling the same ideas effectively. Meditation and mindfulness are other ways to make you comfortable in your daily life. Practicing meditation activities helps you regulate your emotions and center your attention on what you want to do, not ruminating and worrying restlessly. There will be some stuff out of your power. Learning how to understand this will go a long way to prevent overthinking.

Releasing the negative energy inside you is going to be an essential part of becoming a freer person. By infusing your life with positivity, you can live with an open mind and heart that is willing to learn from different situations. Try putting on a happy face. Smile, but do so willfully and cheerfully. Then you can experience what it is like to have fewer worries in your life. Find ways to experience the joy that never goes away. Even if you do not feel happy one day, you will always feel a sense of deep satisfaction, knowing that you are making a meaningful life for yourself on earth, and you are not going to let anything get you down.

This book has walked you through the steps you will need to stop worrying in your life. First, we started by talking about the causes of your mental clutter and what you could do to handle different life situations. We talked about doing less and worrying less, getting rid of your junk, waiting to answer messages, and forgiving the past. Also, we mentioned different ways of dealing with your negative thoughts, which could come and take over your mind at any moment. Additionally, we mentioned how you could practice mindfulness to improve your mood and boost your cognitive performance. We talked about how to determine what is important to you and how to set appropriate goals that would lead you to a happier and more fulfilled place.

As we wrap up this journey and try to defeat the demons within us, we see that there is little that truly needs to be worried. Life is short and swift. One minute we're alive, and the next minute, we are already lying in our graves. I'm sure that before we die, we will regret the times that we have spent worrying about our lives.Life is precious; therefore, we shouldn't waste our time in this world, worrying about things. Although we do not always have it all together, and we sometimes break down and cry and get it all out, that does not mean we stay there. Release the energy within you that is getting you down. Get it all out, and stop worrying. That is a vital part of your future.

Lastly, practicing positive self-talk can transform how you think. Remember, you are what you think. For that reason, if you think positively about yourself, it likely means that you are being the best version of yourself. Eliminate any negative thoughts from your mind by developing a habit of looking at life from a positive perspective. Sure, you can't prevent yourself from thinking negatively all the time. However, it's what you do to manage your negative thoughts that matters the most. Accordingly, stick to the recommended strategies of taming your thoughts discussed in this guide. Mold your life by thinking right. Think of a beautiful life full of hope and optimism. Practice living that life now by doing the things that you would like to do to contribute to a happy and blissful life. Arguably, this is the best way of preventing yourself from experiencing the negative effects of overthinking such as anxiety and stress.

Good luck!

ABOUT THE AUTHOR

John Ward is a professor, a motivational speaker, an author, and holds two degrees in psychology and neuroscience. He has devoted his life to helping people become their best selves both in the classroom and in countless books.

With his background in behavioral sciences and developmental psychology, John has managed to help numerous people overcome their self-defeating habits in order to become better individuals. He has been a star speaker at self-improvement conferences, local centers for the underprivileged, and sometimes even at college graduations. John wishes to help as many people transform their lives for the better before he himself turns fifty years old.

When he's not writing or teaching, John enjoys traveling the world with his adoring wife of almost twenty years by his side. And because John is a family man, first and foremost, he enjoys spending the free time that he has, with his family. He is proud to father two amazing and successful sons, one of whom, wishes to follow in his father's footsteps and become a motivational speaker himself.

REFERENCES

Ali Walker (2017) Get conscious: how to stop over-thinking and come alive. Retrieved from https://www.get-conscious-how-to-stop-overthinking-and-come-alive

Gwendoline Smith (2020) The book of Overthinking: how to stop the cycle of worry. Retrieved from https://www.how-to-stop-the-cycle-of-worry.

Emma S.J. Smith (May 24, 2020) Anxiety in Relationship: How to overcome Anxiety, Jealousy and Negative Thinking to Build a Strong and Healthy Relationship
Retrieved from https://www.anxiety-in-Relationship.

Steven Schuster (2018) Rewire your mind: Stop overthinking. Reduce Anxiety and worrying. Control your thoughts to make better decisions. Retrieved from https://www.rewire-your-mind.

Kirsty Ginman (2008) Be your own confidence coach: Banish self-doubt and boost Self-esteem. Retrieved from https://www.be-your-own-confidence-coach.